Alfredo

Verbal Doodling.

Häberli

*For Stefanie,
Aline, and Luc,
and
for my parents*

Contents

The Lines of My Hand Page 17

Glimpsing a New World Page 21

Can We Count on Chance? Page 28

Dreams are Dependable Page 30

Enzo Mari, the Design Conscience Page 47

Bruno Munari, or: Making Air Visible Page 54

Italo Lupi and the Periodical
as Built Architecture Page 59

Then I Ran out of Breath Page 62

El hombre que me hizo observar el mundo:
Enzo Mari Page 68

Rolf Fehlbaum or
How to Take Pleasure Seriously Page 72

The Friendship with RF,
as We Called Him Page 78

Martin Heller or:
What are You Working On? Page 93

Riccardo Sarfatti, a Beacon of Light Page 96

Renato Stauffacher or
Little, Tiny Sparks of Joy Page 107

Riccardo Blumer and the
Deceptive Lightness of Inquiry Page 118

Contents

Enrico Astori,
at First a Fleeting Encounter   Page 121

Giulio Cappellini,
the Truffle Hound   Page 136

Patrizia Moroso or *buongiorno tesoro*   Page 140

The Invisible Ones —
il famoso ufficio tecnico   Page 146

Konstantin Grcic and Jasper Morrison —
Sketching Our Own Landscape   Page 149

Back to My Friend and Fellow Designer
Konstantin Grcic   Page 158

Anders Byriel or Hygge in Milan   Page 167

Philippe Starck,
l'homme qui ne dort pas la nuit   Page 173

Ross Lovegrove — Supernatural   Page 180

The Journalists —
Word Acrobats and Linguistic Architects   Page 187

Atelier, Studio, Office
as Wunderkammer   Page 192

Bar Basso and Negroni Sbagliato —
The Designers' Cocktail   Page 202

IKEA PS — *La rivoluzione a Milano
siamo noi svedesi*   Page 205

Alfredo Häberli — Verbal Doodling

Amore mio,
Milan and Italy remain my great loves   Page 209

Il consulente   Page 211

Giulio Ridolfo —
Serene Radicalism, Radical Serenity   Page 218

Ramón Úbeda,
Fearless Acrobat and Chameleon   Page 224

Eugenio Perazza,
with Courage and Passion   Page 229

Continuity with Clients or
Endless Lines   Page 232

Mille Miglia, *la corsa più bella de mondo*   Page 234

Hotel Speronari —
l'albergo con vista stelle   Page 240

Fiera Campionaria or
Exhibiting as Memorializing   Page 244

Ettore Sottsass or:
the Inner Life of Restaurants   Page 247

Libreria Internazionale, Ulrico Hoepli —
Libri illeggibili   Page 252

Eleonora Zanotta —
Dream and Reality   Page 255

The Way Things Go   Page 264

Preface

> A pause, a period
> of enforced
> introspection
> that gifted me the time to ask myself:
> Did happiness find me?
> Can we count on chance?
> Are the life lines on my
> palm preordained?
> Has reality really changed
> so much?

Suddenly, everything seemed to stand still. An unbelievable pandemic was sweeping across the world, and with it a visual silence. Thoughts of the past caught up with me anew every day: remembered images, vivid, authentic. I began to write them down, since it is handwriting that actually connects head and hand. I let it happen, this verbal doodling—which was easy in that somnambulant state: watching, heeding my own mind at work in all its banality and complexity.

It was 2020—a year without design. For once there was no Salone del Mobile in Milan. It was the first time I had missed the furniture fair since the start of my student days in 1986, the first year I did not revisit the place where my dreams coalesced and the course of my life was set. This capacity of mine to relive what I felt and thought, what I really wanted and casually took on board, is a wonderful gift in my view. I just let my recollections flow from head to hand with the same lightness of touch as I have when drawing, let myself be repetitive and constantly circle around the same few themes. Manifested in the title, *Non–Random Reminiscences,* in my own, less–than–perfect language, is a kind of verbal doodling informed by a profound sense of gratitude to those people whom I have encountered along the way and who have shaped my life as a designer.

The concentration on Milan as a crucial fork in the road is deliberate. The city left its mark on me in the form of a certain nonchalance, a certain effortlessness, and it was the people I met there, all those encounters, all those dreams, not to mention my own sheer dogged persistence, that spurred me on to write. My life is so much more complex and more varied, and has been shaped by so many more people than those about whom I have written here, but the happiness I chanced on in Milan was most definitely the starting point for the past three decades of my life.

The people who feature in this account, and even more so those who do not, including those who would play a role in my development as a designer only much later, will, I hope, forgive me. After all, this retelling is but a fragment written from a wholly subjective viewpoint, from my own autobiographical memory. And what that memory recalls is the story of how I became a designer—the story I tell myself, that is. Perhaps it did not happen quite like that, but it rings true nonetheless, because what matters most is how these people, and many others like them, fired my imagination, and because I would like to think that I, in my turn, can fire others' imaginations, too.

Verbal Doodling

The Lines of My Hand

Whenever I was not at school, I spent almost all my lunch breaks in the foyer of Kunsthaus Zürich, two streetcar stops away from the architects Marti + Kast and Partner, where from 1980 to 1984 I did an apprenticeship as an architectural draftsman. The museum's annual pass for students was eminently affordable, so I went to all the exhibitions there as well as just stopping by to see the collection—sometimes in depth, sometimes just en passant for inspiration.

One day I happened to pick up a sheet of paper that was lying on the floor of the foyer. It was a flyer for the Berufsmittelschule, a kind of community college that provided further training after vocational school. What struck me, however, was the emphasis given to design. What serendipity! It was like a sign from heaven that was to change my whole life. Back at the architects' office, I asked if I could enroll there. While my immediate supervisor was unresponsive, I did manage to win the support of an older colleague and henceforth spent one day a week attending a three-year design course. This is an opportunity that exists only in Switzerland and it complemented the work of an apprentice draftsman perfectly. My supervisor was not at all pleased and warned me that he would no longer be able to give me such interesting work. His threat backfired, however, as now I was more motivated than ever. I often worked long into the night and even at weekends, which strictly speaking was illegal for us students back then, although I did it of my own accord and never wrote down the hours.

The Gestalterische Berufsmittelschule that I began attending in the second year of my apprenticeship was located on Herostrasse in Altstetten, then still a suburb of Zurich. My subjects were drawing, photography (including film processing), visual design, German, and English. We learned and practiced every conceivable artistic technique, and the longer I was there, the clearer my vocation became. I wanted to become an artist!

So that seemingly trivial act of picking up a piece of litter—that typically Swiss virtue of keeping the public space clean and tidy—in fact marked the first major crossroads of my adult life.

My apprenticeship as an architectural draftsman meant everything to me, and the Berufsmittelschule was heaven! I was surrounded by wonderful people at the office and had excellent teachers at my new school. I was so eager to learn, so open to ideas, so highly motivated that everything seemed easy. It all came so naturally to me. I painted away until late at night, burning the midnight oil, and found a world of my own in architecture, art, and automotive design. The only thing I still missed was the Argentinian mentality, though fortunately for me, the people around me were supportive and indulgent of my extrovert ways. Besides, I was a good apprentice, even if rather headstrong—extremely headstrong, in fact.

Hans Marti was over six feet tall and had a very deep voice. As a planner and co-founder of Marti & Kast Partners, he always wore a suit and tie to work, though politically he was probably left-leaning, given how he stood up for the little villages of Ticino. Nothing and no one escaped his notice. He was already very old when I began my apprenticeship, but when he heard of my wish to go to the Gestalterische Berufsmittelschule he immediately gave me his full support. I had already found someone to champion me, someone of great stature with a deep voice!

When the secretary Miss Rey mentioned to him that I spent my evenings at home painting, he summoned me into his office to ask what kind of paints I was using. My gouaches and acrylic paints did not meet with his approval and he told me that as a beginner I should be finding my way in watercolor. He then sent me out to buy a certain brand of watercolor paints along with the brushes and a block of the right paper, all of which was a present of the studio, he said—though it was also an investment, given that it all cost more than my monthly wage.

From then on, Herr Marti set me assignments to do at home. They were very specific, step–by–step exercises, and if the results were not good enough, he made me do them all over again. And so it went on, day after day, month after month—probably a whole year long. Then one day I happened not to go home at all. I was at an age when much of my mental space was taken up with girls…

Having been unable to do my daily watercolor exercises, I appeared before Herr Marti empty–handed and shamefacedly told him the truth. That time he gave me a second chance, but not a month had passed before the same thing happened again. That was one time too many. I had blown it with Herr Marti! By then I had learned enough to get started, however, and was in any case ready to move on.

Verbal Doodling

Glimpsing a New World

The girl I really wanted to have as a girlfriend back then had a sister whose boyfriend, Martin Greenland, was doing a summer internship with the architects Esther and Rudolf Guyer at the Römerhof in Zurich, just 200 meters from Marti & Kast Partners. We agreed to meet up one day and thanks to him some completely new names came to my attention. Not only did he open my eyes to the world of the Architectural Association (AA) in London, where he was studying under professors like James "Big Jim" Stirling, the man who built the Staatsgalerie Stuttgart and won great acclaim for it as a shining example of postmodernist design, but he also talked of Nigel Coates, Rem Koolhaas, and Zaha Hadid, who at the time were assistants at the AA; it was also through him that I discovered Coop Himmelb(l)au and Hans Hollein in Vienna. Martin became not just a friend, but also a partner with whom I was able to enter competitions that I had never heard of and would not normally have been eligible for: one for the London–based *The Architecture Review* and, later, one for the Milanese design journal *Domus*. Those competition projects became an exciting nighttime and weekend activity for me—

alongside the painting exercises. This really was a new world. We were naive and bursting with hope, and one time even managed to get a drawing of ours published.

As eager as I was to see more of this world and to become part of it, I first had to finish my apprenticeship. Meanwhile, my older sister Laura had bought herself a VW Golf GTI. This was the first Golf, the one designed by Giorgietto Giugiaro, and I just loved its angularity. The first time we took it for a spin we drove to Ticino. All that mattered was to go somewhere warmer, further south, a little bit more like Argentina, which after all is home to eight million second-generation Italians, meaning that almost every Italian has relatives there. We reached the Italian border in no time and decided to continue on to Milan. Now, the Italian approach to traffic is very different than the Swiss, and not just in relation to traffic signals; the driving style and treatment of pedestrians are similarly incompatible and it can seem as if there are completely different laws in force. As Laura knew only the Swiss highway code and had not been driving long, especially not with her nice new car, she asked me to take over at the wheel instead—and I didn't even have a driver's license!

Alfredo Häberli

By the time we parked the coupé with the golf-ball gearstick and red-rimmed radiator grille not far from Milan Cathedral, our nerves were severely frayed. We had bitten off way more than we could chew and were too exhausted to do anything but sleep. Fortunately, Martin had told me of a hotel where he and the other AA students had stayed on a class trip not long before. The name of the hotel was the same as the street on which it was located and after an hour or so of looking we finally found it: Hotel Speronari on Via Speronari.

The entrance to the hotel was on Via Speronari, a narrow side street off Via Torino close to Piazza del Duomo. Next to the hotel was a little greengrocer's that was open from early in the morning until late at night. To reach the first-floor reception desk you had to climb a very narrow flight of stairs, so narrow that it would have been almost impossible to get a suitcase up there.

"Buona sera," said the friendly man at reception, and then asked us how many hours we would be staying. My Italian was not great, but Italian was close enough to Spanish for me to understand well enough. "How many hours?! The whole night of course! Until tomorrow morning." We then gave him our passports and asked to have two separate rooms. "Two rooms?!" he asked incredulously, hastily adding, "I don't need your passports. And I'll give you a good price since you're staying so long—if you pay cash in advance, that is." We found our tiny little rooms two floors further up. Soon afterwards, when my sister and I were talking to each other on the internal telephone—both of us being too lazy to get up—we soon realized that we could converse perfectly well without it. The walls were paper–thin.

We also heard a door open and shut. And then the rhythmic squeaking of bedsprings: a couple having sex—tempestuous and short. Then the door opened and shut again—as it would all through the night. It was comical, loud, and embarrassing. I was ashamed for my sister's sake. What kind of a place was this? The price had been very reasonable. Was that because of all the noise? Why hadn't Martin warned me? Eventually I fell asleep and let my dreams take over.

I was roused by the sound of men talking loudly in the corridor. Was it a gang? My sister had woken up, too, and after agreeing that we should leave the hotel at once we began dressing hastily. The men were in fact a team of builders who communicated by shouting—from room to room, from floor to floor. They were working there as part of the team that was fixing up the hotel, and consequently were amazed to discover us there. "What are you two up to?" they sniggered.

Once out on the street again, the penny finally dropped: Evidently the hotel was renting out rooms by the hour, but only at night when the builders were not there. How clever—and how brazen. So that was why the man at reception had looked at us in such astonishment! Mr. and Mrs. Häberli—he must have thought, looking at our passports—wanting separate rooms for the night? What kind of a weird relationship was that? No sex?!

Off we went, wandering aimlessly through the streets looking for the car—and then discovered to our horror that the brand-new Golf GTI was no longer there! That was too much for my sister. She had saved up for years to buy it. We might just as well have been in Argentina. What idiots we had been! In Italy, too, it seemed, you couldn't just drive up in your fancy new car and park it wherever you liked. And I had so much wanted to show my sister Milan! The Milan of Hotel Speronari? And now the car gone!

A waiter appeared in front of the bar on the opposite side of the street. "Buongiorno signorina. Buongiorno giovanotto. Un caffè? Offro io." My sister was still sobbing. "What's happened?" asked the waiter. "How can I help?" So we told him what had happened, and he told us that just half an hour earlier, a black car with a Swiss license plate had been towed away from that very same spot, because there was no parking allowed on that side of the street. He advised us to make inquiries of the Polizia Municipale on Via Cesare Beccaria. What a relief that was. Perhaps it would turn out all right after all. "Would you now like a coffee? It'll be my treat," he said. And while we were drinking his espresso, he explained which way we had to go. We were still dead tired, but set off for Via Cesare Beccaria without delay, arriving just in time to see the tow truck unloading the black VW Golf GTI with that familiar Swiss license plate. The relief was written all over Laura's face. The next two hours were spent on bureaucracy, by the end of which my sister was 355,000 lire (350 euros) poorer, though at least she had her new car back. After that nightmare, we were ready to head for home. Driving back, we hardly talked at all and for a long time the only sound was the gentle purring of the engine. It took a while before we could see the funny side of it.

Alfredo Häberli

The renovated Hotel Speronari on Via Speronari was for many years my go-to address in Milan. It was ideally situated, good value, and I could be sure of always getting the same room: the only room with a terrace and a view of the bells of the Chiesa di Santa Maria presso San Satiro. The only downside was that the bathroom and shower were an experiment from the 1970s made entirely of plastic and extremely small. To take a shower you first had to slide the basin over the toilet bowl, as only then was there space enough to stand, even if the whole room got a sprinkling.

Over the years, however, I got so adept at handling this that it became a kind of ritual. It also taught me the importance of doing things in the right order.

Later still, Hotel Speronari became the hotel where I accommodated my assistants during the Salone del Mobile and where I always prebooked ten rooms to distribute among my designer friends. Konstantin Grcic and his assistants once stayed there, for example. Yet since it was still basically a student hostel with just one and a half stars, I never breathed a word of this to my customers. Sometimes I called it the "Spermanari"—a joke that only my sister and I understood.

Can We Count on Chance?

Verbal Doodling

Milan became my substitute for Argentina. I went there regularly and it was there that I discovered the world of design. That, too, was by chance—or rather by being observant, by searching. I kept on running into this nice old gentleman with a wrinkled face grinning back at me from a black–and–white photograph. The photo was among those to feature on the labels dangling from the products in the furniture showrooms that I was so busy devouring. It was all so new to me; but I was curious, and courageous enough to go in and have a look around. The purpose of the faces on the labels nevertheless eluded me. What was the point of that?

Only later did I learn that the photos were of the designers who had created the items to which they were attached. The only ones I knew were Pierre Cardin, from my father, and Pininfarina, a car designer whom my father and uncle were constantly talking about. But that a person could design a chair, a lamp, an armchair—that was new to me. My vision of the future crystallized a little more sharply with each new visit to Milan.

Alfredo Häberli

I immersed myself in the world of things, of objects, of Achille Castiglioni with his *Caccia* and *Toio* lamps, his *Cumano* table and *Mezzadro* stool, and in the showrooms of Cassina and Flos in Milan! Then I discovered Paolo Piva's *Arcada* desk, Antonio Citterio and Paolo Nava's *Diesis* sofa for B&B, Giovanni Offredi's *Wave* chairs for Saporiti, and later Mario Botta's *Seconda* chair, Richard Sapper's *Tizio* lamp for Artemide, the famous *Wink* armchair, and the *Veranda* sofa. For me it was all a dream come true and a revelation of what I wanted to do with my life. My own dream began: the dream that one day, the black-and-white portrait photo on the object label would be mine.

Dreams are Dependable

Verbal Doodling

Just a few hundred meters behind Zurich Main Station is one of the finest examples of modernist architecture in Switzerland. Set in a park with a pond, it is an L–shaped complex that houses both the Museum für Gestaltung (Museum of Design), formerly the Kunstgewerbemuseum (Museum of Arts and Crafts), and the Schule für Gestaltung (School of Design), formerly the Kunstgewerbeschule (School of Arts and Crafts). The building alone held a particular fascination for me right from the start, though whether because of its proportions, its sleekness, or the rationality of the whole conception I cannot say.

That I wanted to become a designer was growing ever more apparent. When I told my parents of this wish, they were not in the least surprised. My father just remarked that he himself had had no choice, and that with four children to feed he had had to go into business, even if he would have liked to pursue a more artistic path. He added that as attractive as the profession of designer was, it would require great persistence. My mother worried more about how we were going to finance it. As children we had always been invited to express an opinion and had been given a say in family decision–making

Alfredo Häberli

from a very young age. Our dinner table was a scene of democracy in action, which is why the ritual of eating together was so important to my parents. Mealtimes were when everyone was heard and all sorts of things discussed. Sometimes we even voted. The day of that memorable conversation when I consulted my mother and father on my own future was the day I realized that I was now grown–up and that my parents took me seriously. I knew I had their full moral support.

At the Berufsmittelschule where I was taking a preparatory course in design, it was my professors who encouraged me to pursue my chosen path. Hearing that the Schule für Gestaltung offered a course in interior architecture and product design, I had them send me a prospectus and application form and decided to sign up for the entrance exam without doing the foundation course first. But before I could do that, I first had to complete my apprenticeship as an architectural draftsman and to pass the written and practical exams for the Berufsmittelschule.

My written project was about the sculptures of Raffael Benazzi, a Swiss artist with a studio on Wasserwerkstrasse on the River Limmat, not far from Escher–Wyss–Platz. Benazzi's studio was always open to me and I was fortunate in being able to get to know this interesting artist personally—as well as his wife and daughter, whom I dated briefly. After one of my visits, moreover, Benazzi took me with him to the opening of an exhibition by a woman artist who happened to be a friend of his. The venue was at the Römerhof, very close to Marti & Kast Partners.

On arriving there, my mentor introduced me as a young student and then left me to my own devices. I was standing there cluelessly amid all these vaguely familiar people when the elderly artist herself came over and began talking to me—and we got on like a house on fire! Her curiosity was exceptional, and although the questions I asked her were naive, she seemed not to care. Her name did not mean anything to me at the time, and she must have noticed that, but she still seemed happy to be chatting to me.

That encounter stayed with me for a long while, as it turned out that I had missed something fundamental, namely that the lady in question was Meret Oppenheim, in those days Switzerland's most famous living artist! Years later, I was perusing a secondhand bookstore when I chanced on a copy of *Domus* No. 605 with Meret Oppenheim on the cover. That stuck in my mind, and I still have the magazine in my library today. Those portraits of great artists and designers that graced the covers of *Domus* for a while impressed me no end, just as that black-and-white photo of Achille Castiglione had. I can still see them in my mind's eye: Mario Merz, Aldo Rossi, Enzo Mari, the *imprenditore* Aurelio Zanotta, and Piero Busnelli in his dandyish white suit. Those issues, and many others, too, were to have an enduring impact on me.

As my girlfriend in those days lived in Ascona, I saw her only every few days, when she helped out her mother at Café Steinwies, just one stop away from the architects' office. Every month she brought me the latest edition of *Domus* from Italy—and wrote endearing little messages on the ads for me to discover later on.

Whenever I stopped by the offices of the Schule für Gestaltung, which I did all the time in the mid–1980s, I had to first walk past the foyer of the design museum and then past the library into the school. It was there that I once spotted Achille Castiglioni himself coming down the stairs into the main hall. I'd only ever seen his face in the photos adorning the Zanotta products and had not known how small he was. Nor had I ever witnessed his witty, slapstick–style body movements, and propensity to gesticulate. The exhibition *Achille Castiglioni, Designer* that ran from February 6 to March 31, 1985 opened just a short time later, unfurling before me on a thousand square meters of exhibition space the Castiglioni brothers' whole cosmos. It was a dream come true—my life, my future, spread out before me.

Ten years later I curated and designed the exhibition *Bruno Munari—Far vedere l'Aria* in that very same space. And ten years later still I was able to fill the hall with my own work in the exhibition *SurroundThings*. In retrospect, it is as if my fate had been mapped out for me all along. Only there were to be days, months, years of hard grind before then.

To return to my hopes of a place at the Schule für Gestaltung: The entrance exam was held over a three–day period. There were over two hundred candidates, but just twelve places. The tasks they set us were exacting, but exciting and stimulating, too—pure adrenaline. For me it was a question of to be or not to be: to be one of the lucky twelve, or not. But I went into it feeling pretty confident. To start with we were given a 50 × 70–centimeter sheet of paper, out of which we had to build a bridge strong enough to support a tube of glue and high enough for the tube to pass under it. Then we had to draw a brick, and to describe a brick in German. There was some arithmetic, too, and some other tasks that no longer spring to mind. Three whole days. An exhilarating experience! I'd never been anxious about exams. For me they were always a challenge that I was happy to take. Besides, I wanted to know where I stood, how I measured up. I had finished the Berufsmittelschule and my apprenticeship with flying colors, and that gave me confidence.

All the more devastating was the news that I had come thirteenth. That was a terrible blow and caught me unawares, especially as I had already planned to use the time remaining between the exam and the start of the academic year to visit my beloved Argentina. After a lot of pleading, I was at least granted an audience. It turned out that anyone in the top thirty was entitled to a hearing and that was an offer I gladly took up.

The professor I talked to was very kind and solicitous, but he also delivered the most damning verdict imaginable: a rejection—not by much, but still indubitably a rejection. I had not been admitted to the interior architecture and product design course. I also learned that I had lost a lot of points on my German, which was the one thing I could not do well. German, after all, is not my mother tongue. I was deeply disappointed and raged at the unfairness of it all. But with my flight departing just a few hours later there was no time for sentimentality. I used the enforced idleness on the plane to Buenos Aires Ezeiza to compose a letter to Alf Aebershold, the professor who had had to relay the painful news of my rejection to me; and I even managed to persuade one of the air hostesses to take the letter and mail it for me on her return to Switzerland. That was strictly against cabin–crew rules; after all, the envelope might have contained something explosive. The contents were indeed explosive—or so it felt to me; and I didn't even have a stamp to hand.

But I had to get the disappointment, the indignation, off my chest, and to protest that my inadequacies in German were not my fault. I had never suffered any setbacks prior to that. I had never had a plan B. And now I was going to be traveling for several weeks, meaning that the chances of being offered a spot were minimal. I had come thirteenth and that was that.

On returning home to Zurich, the official rejection letter was waiting for me. It was hardly a consolation, but it did at least galvanize me into setting off in search of work. So with my portfolio tucked under my arm, I visited the ten best architects' offices in Zurich, including Fritz Schwarz, Bétrix & Consolascio, Ueli Marbach and Arthur Rüegg, and Robert and Trix Haussmann. I knew them only from *werk, bauen + wohnen* and *Archithese,* the magazines that my former employer had subscribed to, and had been able to find only the Haussmanns' private address, not that of their studio, which I later found out was called the Allgemeine Entwurfsanstalt on Höschgasse. Their private address was just around the corner, between the Pavillon Le Corbusier and the studio.

On the way there I happened to see a sign saying "AH & P"—my very own initials!—and with typical Argentinian chutzpah spontaneously rang the doorbell. I was greeted by a person who introduced himself as Walter, which happens to be my middle name. After viewing my portfolio, however, the owner of the initials, Andy Hauser, told me that I was overqualified for what they did, which was basically display window design, and that I should instead try my luck with the interior designer on the top floor of the same building.

There I encountered a man with a broken leg that he was keeping elevated on a lectern. I showed him my portfolio and he asked me if I could drive and whether I was free that afternoon. Yes, I could drive, I said, and all that I had planned for that afternoon was to show my portfolio to as many studios as possible. I was eager to work and earn money. Half an hour later I had been hired, and on excellent wages too! My most pressing problem had been solved and I was ready to accompany my new boss to the site of his current project. I still called in at the Allgemeine Entwurfsanstalt, which was just 100 meters down the road, and there was greeted by Stefan Zwicky, whom I would get to know properly only many years later, and who told me they were not looking for anyone at present. I also had an interesting conversation with Bétrix & Consolascio, but of course by then I already had a job.

As my workload was not enough to fill the whole day, I decided to sit in on some architecture courses at the Eidgenössische Technische Hochschule (ETH Zürich, the Swiss Institute of Technology). It was actually a great year and extremely eye-opening. The lectures of the legendary René Furer deepened my knowledge of architectural theory as well as satisfying my

Alfredo Häberli

curiosity. Furer typically rattled through two whole drums of slides and set my retina ablaze with images and stories of buildings from all over the world. He was stimulating and at times incomprehensible, but always witty and eloquent, as in his maxim: "A photo is more reliable than a plan or the written word and ideal for the impatient." Perhaps it was Furer's style of delivery that inspired me always to include images in my own lectures. The history of art and architecture was taught by Professor Werner Oechslin, while Professor Peter Jenny was responsible for visual design.

At last it was time to retake the entrance exam for the Schule für Gestaltung, as my dream had not changed since the previous summer. This time, however, I was familiar with the procedure and knew what awaited me. I was also working on the project in Zug and had to visit the building site first thing in the morning before going back to Zurich for the exam. Perhaps because of that I went into the exam feeling a lot less positive, but also caring less than I had the first time around. Then came the good news: I had been admitted! I again wanted to know why and again requested a consultation. This time it was with Professor Franco Clivio, who pulled no punches when he assured me that my German was as execrable as ever. Yet the very fact that I had retaken the exam had shown how determined I was. Second attempts were apparently very unusual in those days. I felt as if I'd been cheated out of a whole year and defiantly swore to myself: I'll show you!

As the interior designers wanted me to continue supplying them with ideas, I decided to keep my job and do it in the evenings after school. On our first day at the Schule für Gestaltung, all twelve of us freshmen were asked why we were there. The answers were almost all the same: to get a better job and earn more money. I was shocked. Surely design is a calling, I thought, and phrased my own response accordingly. Compared to the entrance exam, the course itself was very, very slow, and almost boring at times. Most of my surplus energy went into my evening job and into the idea of organizing a series of lectures like the ones I had attended at the ETH's Hönggerberg campus. This my fellow students and I eventually succeeded in doing with a first series by architects (including Jacques Herzog, Santiago Calatrava, and Peter and Jörg Quarella) in 1986 and a second by designers in 1987. We did it all ourselves, from the initial contact and official invitation to the formal introduction and moderation of the Q & A session.

The library at the Schule für Gestaltung was an Aladdin's cave for me. Some of the books had to be ordered up from the stacks, while others we were allowed to fetch ourselves. There were also sloping desks with an array of magazines laid out on them, and no end of books. In Milan it was the objects that were my world, in Zurich it was the library—a world that took me into the past, into the history of design.

So that was another way of taking advantage of the sluggish tempo. One day in my first year, I learned that there was an annual furniture fair in Milan. I already knew the city a little—the showrooms around the Piazza San Babila and Hotel Speronari—so felt confident about asking my tutor if I could go to Milan for three days. Sure, he said, the Salone del Mobile would count as an educational trip. All I had to do was submit a request six months in advance. That, of course, was impossible, as I had intended to go the very next day. Insolent as I was, I gave him a choice: He should let me go or I would undoubtedly fall sick. He gave in to my demand, asking only that it remain our little secret. So off I went, taking two friends along with me: Michael Heimgartner and Christian Droz.

If I remember rightly, it was in September 1986, after the summer vacation, that I first went to the Milan furniture fair and first saw all those presentations in the galleries, palazzos, abattoirs, showrooms, and fair booths. It was crazy! A total dream world that was so utterly unlike what I was being taught and what I was learning from books and so much closer to the magical world I had glimpsed in the magazines. I saw Jasper Morrison's *Thinking Man's Chair,* the Pallucco exhibition at the old slaughterhouse or *macellaio,* and Shiro Kuramata's show with red lasers and music from Andrey Tarkovsky's movie *Stalker.* Then there were the first presentations by Phillippe Starck with Baleri and Driade, the showrooms by Cassina, Achille Castiglioni, and Vico Magistretti, and so much more besides.

And although we were just students, we were chauffeured around in dark blue limousines, which was all part of the service. The only way to obtain information in those days was to talk to people face to face, to ask them questions, exchange ideas. We were given addresses and lists of the must–see shows and events, all of which was simply *impensabile!* I greedily drank it all in, and then some. It was like getting high without drugs, and it instantly became my drug of choice. From then on, I made a point of going to Milan for my annual shot of delirium. It was only later that I felt sick to my stomach—cooped up in those narrow corridors, working on assignments in design history, which of course went from the Bauhaus to the Hochschule für Gestaltung (HfG) Ulm, reaching its zenith in "form follows function." I gave talks on Jean Paul Gaultier and Shiro Kuramata and took a personal interest in the works of Pallucco and Zeus, and the *Wohnen von Sinnen* books. It was wild stuff—incomprehensible, resistant to any rational explanation. I had no words for it, could not make sense of what I was seeing, but desperately wanted to understand it. Yet I was also enthralled by the works of Jacob Müller, Wilhelm Kienzle, Hans Hilfiker, and the anonymous design of Swiss history generally.

My professors were worried that I would rush to do whatever was fashionable, that I would be all too easily led astray. But this was my world, this was Milan, the world of Achille Castiglioni, that bizarre world that had made him so strong. The world of trends, of fashion, of postmodernism was undoubtedly interesting and transparent, but it was not mine, even if it gave me scope to play around and opened up new perspectives.

I expended a good deal of energy during those first two years at the Schule für Gestaltung, but was alienated by what I was unearthing. Where was I? What was my own stance? What were my own interests? My professors turned out to be right. I was confused. Hence my decision to do an internship in hopes of gaining some perspective and finding myself again. I wanted to go as far away as possible, to Japan, where my ambition was to work for Shiro Kuramata in Tokyo. My tutor agreed to the idea on condition that I return. By then he knew that I kept my promises and so was ready to let me go.

But I did not have anything concrete to offer as an intern, and Kuramata in any case turned me down, explaining in his letter—which I still have—that his office was so tiny that even he had to fold up his table to get inside, and that he did not speak any language other than Japanese. I might have guessed as much. My professor then helped me out by organizing an internship with Nick Roericht, whose work was more theoretical in thrust, but whose studio was inside the former HfG Ulm, the famous design school co-founded by Max Bill, who for many years had been its director. In the end, I made it to Siemens in New York, though it cost me an arm and a leg to get there. The team was small, just four people, and the work was all in the field of telecommunications and medical apparatus. Luckily, I was able to move into an apartment on Spring and Lafayette. The only person I knew prior to my arrival, and then only by fax, was Jonas Milder, the man who headed Nick Roericht's office in New York City.

My roommate was unemployed at the time and took it upon himself to show me as many of New York's galleries, museums, and discos as possible. The Donald Judd Building was just a few blocks away and I once even saw him there, though otherwise it looked deserted. A friend of Jonas Milder's in Brooklyn had been commissioned to make wooden furniture for Judd, as had Milder himself once or twice. I also saw the first Donald Judd retrospective at the Cooper Hewitt Museum. Back on an even keel, I began discovering New York City, which for me was the Leo Castelli Gallery, the Storefront for Art and Architecture, the Printed Matter bookstore, Pearl Paint, and of course the museums. I got to see architecture shows about Diller Scofidio and Krueger Kaplan, performances by Peter Wilson, and concerts by David Byrne, Talking Heads, and Laurie Anderson.

As much as I enjoyed broadening my horizons in New York, I was also eager to complete my design diploma, especially as the Schule für Gestaltung was unique in having both a museum and a design school under one roof. What luxury! So I returned to Switzerland and henceforth savored every month, every day, every hour in which I was able to get to grips with design. I knew even then how important self–knowledge is. The key questions underlying all independent work will always be:

Who am I? What do I want?

Verbal Doodling

Enzo Mari, the Design Conscience

My habit of walking from Bruno Munari's studio in the Wagner–Buonarroti district to Hotel Speronari became something of a ritual and helped me to process the archived materials that I had just viewed. A few months earlier— this was in 1993—I had suggested to the Museum für Gestaltung Zürich that it stage an exhibition on Bruno Munari and Enzo Mari. The show was to be based on the collection of Bruno Danese and Jacqueline Vodoz, the proprietors of Danese of Milan, a small but important producer of home décor.

It was at a dinner party at the Daneses that I first met Renato Minetto, the editor and publisher of *Abitare,* among other publications, who turned out to be a great fan of Buenos Aires and a passionate tango dancer. Minetto had asked the magazine's director and graphic designer, Italo Lupi, to find out what I was up to and what I was currently working on, and Lupi, in his turn, had invited me to show the people at *Abitare* my work whenever I was next in Milan. As everyone in those days introduced themselves with a slide show of their work, at least in New York City, I took my slides out of the Kodak Carousel (designed by Hans Gugelot, 1963) and transferred them to a display case made of hard plastic, which I had purchased at Pearl Paint, the huge, five-story-high art supplies store on Canal Street.

On arriving at the editorial offices of *Abitare* at Corso Monforte 15—now the location of the Flos showroom and opposite it the Kvadrat showroom that in 2007 I would be commissioned to remodel—I was welcomed with open arms not just by Lupi, but also by Silvia Latis, Stefano Casciani, and even Marco Romanelli, if I remember rightly. They phoned for some coffee from the bar across the street and then, after briefly holding my slide case up to the light, took it over to the light table to take a closer look. The works I had done as a student were okay, they said, but what interested Lupi were my works as an exhibition architect for the Museum für Gestaltung. It was the graphics and the design work that captivated him, that being something that he and Achille Castiglioni had done for various exhibitions. The Museum für Gestaltung Zürich had an incredible reputation even then, and with Martin Heller as lead curator, and soon to be director, was at the top of its game. The famous Achille Castiglioni exhibition originally conceived in Vienna had been shown there in 1985, a year before Heller's arrival.

Alfredo Häberli

Lupi looked closely at the very different exhibitions that I had designed to date, many of them in part simply to earn money to help me finance the design diploma I was doing inside that very same building. That encounter with Lupi gave rise to an eight-page article by Casciani, who knew the museum well and had an instant grasp of what we in Zurich were up to.

Anyway, there I was in Milan, strolling across town along Via Vittoria Colonna, past the Ristorante Novecento to Corso Vercelli and Corso Magenta, and from there along Via Santa Maria Fulcorina to Via Speronari—about half an hour's walk all in all—when I spotted something that made me stop dead in my tracks. It was a sign that read "Piazzale Baracca," a name that somehow rang a bell. Had I passed the same address earlier that morning? Or had I seen it on a street plan of Milan? But then I saw the number 10 and rushed over to the door to check the names next to the doorbells; and there it was: "Studio Enzo Mari." My heart was beating like crazy and I could no longer think straight. My finger pressed the doorbell as if by remote control and after a few, achingly long, seconds a woman's voice asked how she could help me. Thrown for a loop, I inquired if I might see Mr. Enzo Mari, and was told that no, he was too busy. What was it about, she wanted to know. "I've come all the way from Switzerland specially to deliver something to him in person," I lied—and was all the more astonished when the receptionist, who had wondered out loud why I had not made an appointment in advance, told me to wait a moment. After what again seemed like an eternity, the voice returned with clear instructions. I was to take the elevator at the end of the hall and press the button for the third floor.

I was in! But what was this personal item that I had promised to deliver? Panic set in. I scrabbled around in my bag and found only a Toblerone bar! How ashamed I felt! When I exited the elevator, the door was already open. A young woman ushered me in and offered me a seat in the form of an *Autoprogettazione* chair *No. 1!* It had quite a patina and might even have been the original chair of 1973. I chose to remain standing. After quite a wait, Enzo Mari himself came around the corner holding a piece of licorice. He was clad in corduroys, a sloppy jacket, and rather inelegant leather shoes. His expression was fierce as if slightly annoyed, which he might well have been given that I had interrupted his work. I introduced myself as a young designer currently in the process of preparing an exhibition. He listened attentively, looking sterner by the minute, and then calmly bade me follow him into his study. What happened next would shape my relationship with him for years to come. Not only did he launch into a lecture on design, but he also harangued me for my presumption: I had no business calling myself a designer! I knew too little of the world for that. I was simply too young. That was the hammer. Next came the sickle to cut me down to size.

His desk was strewn with drawings, sheets of paper, and trays labeled IN and OUT, and there were some animals from the *16 Animali* puzzle lying around as well as other industrial objects being used as paperweights. Mari went over to his blackboard and drew some diagrams that I understood only in part, having long since exhausted my knowledge of Italian. On the other hand, I knew his work well, which he noticed right away and evidently found flattering, though he admitted as much only years later. After two hours of this I was unceremoniously shown the door. And it was then that he asked "What was it you had to deliver to me in person?"—whereupon I gave him the Toblerone bar. He was about to launch into another lecture about Switzerland and Swiss industry and chocolate, but apparently thought better of it. Best of all, though, was that having warned me not to burst in on him like that, he asked me to be sure to make an appointment *next time*.

Back on the Piazzale Baracca I continued my stroll, but now with a spring in my step and my head full of ideas. I decided to stop and have a drink at the Bar Magenta, where, typically for Italy, there were all sorts of delicious nibbles laid out on the counter. So that, too, became a ritual. A while later, looking up from making notes in my sketchbook, I saw Enzo Mari himself walk by on the other side of the street—fortunately without noticing me. I watched him pass the Ristorante ai 3 Fratelli at Via Terraggio 11/13 and greet the landlord there—one of the eponymous three brothers—and promptly resolved that this eatery "con specialità toscane, con aria condizionata e giardino estivo" would become one of my haunts, too. Enzo Mari lived just around the corner and his terrace full of bonsais actually looked out onto the restaurant. The landlord assured me that the *professore* walked by at the same time every day, which was important for me to know. Perhaps I could engineer a "chance" encounter. I so looked forward to one day seeing Enzo Mari walk by again! That was one of my happiest times in Milan. Not only did I know the products, the objects, and the books, but I knew the people behind them, too, and within just a few weeks I had been able to meet first Bruno Munari and then Enzo Mari.

Bruno Munari, or: Making Air Visible

Verbal Doodling

My meeting with Bruno Munari and his wife Dilma was an official one. As I was co-curating the Museum für Gestaltung's forthcoming Bruno Munari exhibition together with Claude Lichtenstein, it was essential that I get to meet the man himself. Bruno and Dilma were so amiable, warm-hearted, open-minded, funny, witty, and on the ball, that within seconds of meeting them I knew this was going to be a wonderful, magical exhibition. Bruno's character guaranteed it.

Since extravagant holidays were out of our reach in the early days of the studio, Stefanie and I often spent our vacations near Lugano in Italian-speaking Switzerland, where in the 1970s her grandparents had built a beautifully situated house. The location had the added advantage of bringing me close to Milan and to my first customers.

Dilma Carnevali Munari and Bruno Munari had a holiday home of their own on Lake Como, which is where they escaped to in the hot summer months—and not just then. One summer, when I was still busy with the research in preparation for the exhibition, Stefanie and I visited them there. We had agreed to meet at

Alfredo Häberli

the Crotto del Lupo, a little restaurant built into a grotto in the hillside and hence the perfect place to have lunch on a hot summer day. Dilma and Bruno were already there when we pulled up in our bright–blue Fiat 128. The blue of the car we had inherited from Stefanie's great-aunt matched the color of the sky so exactly that when viewed against it, it became almost transparent. Whereas the classic limousine outline and the wheels were clearly visible, the body itself seemed to disappear into thin air.

Once we were seated at the table, the waiter came over to give us the menu and take our orders for drinks. And that is when it started: "Here are the menus," he said. "What would you like to drink?" "Water both still and sparkling," replied Munari in his soft but clear voice, "and then we'll take the house wine. A bottle of yellow." "Oh, I'm sorry, Mr. Munari," said the waiter, thinking he might have misheard him, "we have only red or white." "As in white as milk or snow? As in red as strawberries?" asked Munari. That question left the poor waiter lost for words, and to judge by his face, he couldn't quite believe his ears. "As I said, we only have white or red!" he stammered, whereupon Munari relented: "All right, then bring me one of those colors," he said, and the bewildered waiter withdrew.

How splendid it looked from up here: our little sky-blue four-door parked on the gravel parking lot! And that this was the first car to have a plastic radiator grille spray-painted to look like metal made it extra special. The bottle of white—or was it yellow?—arrived and at first the waiter seemed to have forgotten the previous dialogue. But when he pulled out his notepad to take our orders, Bruno, without so much as glancing at the menu, quietly asked him, "Do you have Uova allo spiedo?" No, they did not, the waiter snapped, prompting the next impossible request: "Then bring me a Brodo alla Griglia." That was too much for the exasperated waiter. "We only have what's on the menu!" he wailed. "Please read it and call me when you're ready to order!" And he once again withdrew, this time with a face that really was as red as strawberries.

That was a very amusing lunch that we had at the Crotto. But since we also wanted to discuss some matters relating to the exhibition, we later went to the Munaris' holiday home on the opposite side of the gravel parking lot on which our Fiat was standing—our Fiat, the color of the Argentinian flag and of the *Albiceleste*. On entering the front garden, Dilma, who was clearly exhausted by the heat, turned to her husband and said, "Bruno, why don't you get some air circulating here?" Bruno then opened the garden gate with its vertical iron bars and let Dilma and Stefanie enter first. "Thank you," said Dilma, "what a lovely cool breeze." That kind of witty banter, that kind of subtle wordplay, was typical of Bruno and Dilma. It was always wonderfully spontaneous, never put on. Of course, it sounds a lot more poetic in Italian—and is actually untranslatable. That was also one of the difficulties that Claude Lichtenstein and I had when working on the catalogue of *Far vedere l'Aria,* which is why we left the poems and prose in the original. Wordplay, puns, and ambiguity are very difficult to translate.

It was at that same lunch, incidentally, that I realized that I would have to have two exhibitions: one just for Bruno Munari and a later one dedicated to Enzo Mari. Would the Museum für Gestaltung understand my decision? Would I also have the absolution of Jacqueline Vodoz–Danese and Bruno Danese, on whose collection the Munari exhibition was to be based? The preparations dragged on and I discovered more and more material, as well as other collectors. One advantage of the delay, however, was that in the end we were able to show the exhibition in the main hall of the museum.

Best of all was that Bruno Munari let me have the run of his whole studio, allowing me to sift through everything from top left to bottom right. I discovered holiday postcards from the Maris, letters from Saul Steinberg, letters from architects, artists, and collectors, fine pencil drawings, collages, and prints, and of course copious notes. Huge discoveries!

My Milan and my world were indeed "making the air visible."

Verbal Doodling

Italo Lupi and the Periodical as Built Architecture

Italo Lupi once told me that he, too, went to Milan because of Bruno Munari, just as I did back then. I saw myself reflected in Lupi. Like me, he enjoyed shaping things, making things, playing, observing, and not just for himself, but for others, too, since as art director of *Domus* and director and art director of *Abitare* he was responsible for both the content and the graphic design. It was exhibitions that had lured him away from architecture to graphic design, which also explains why he was so delighted with my own trajectory. There were certainly similarities. I, too, had studied architecture first and later financed my design diploma by creating exhibitions for the Museum für Gestaltung Zürich; and then, of course, there was the inspiration of Achille Castiglioni, with whom he had created so many different exhibitions, not to forget the artist and cartoonist Saul Steinberg, for whom he had designed a show at the Milan Triennale.

It was again Italo Lupi—a man who went around with colored felt tips in his breast pocket, who dressed very much in the English style and almost always wore a tie, who was always amiable, always smiling, always had a wonderfully subtle sense of humor to hand, who was always surrounded by pretty female assistants, and who often had his wife Maria Louisa accompany him—this *architetto* Italo Lupi who published the first major article about my exhibition designs in the magazine *Abitare*. That article was to change the course of my life as a young designer, and not just in Milan, but throughout Italy and even worldwide. Both *Domus* and *Abitare* in those days had a formative impact on the world of architecture and design, and their articles were written by very good journalists and hence properly researched and widely read.

Even today, Lupi still sends me one of the calendars that he and the Grafiche Mariano printing house produce with such passion every year. It used to arrive just before the summer, then in the spring, and the most recent one, for 2019/20, in January. These calendars have since become collector's items and I have kept them all. I used to have them hanging in the workshop, but have since archived them in the drawers of my filing cabinet, along with that first article about me published by Lupi and his team. As Lupi himself once said, "that's

Alfredo Häberli

how we changed the periodical and at the same time kept the memory of its history, its seriousness, and its independence alive. For me, therefore, the sixteen years that I spent as editor of *Abitare* were not just an exceptional time of experimentation and editorial license (aided by a lively, intelligent, cultivated, and productive editorial team), but above all a kind of nursery for nurturing the new shoots being put forth by young and as yet unknown designers (architects, photographers, illustrators, writers). We helped them to the fame they enjoy today, and at the same time turned the spotlight on those great masters of the past who in the meantime had been largely forgotten."

He loved the tie–in book for the exhibition *Bruno Munari—Far vedere l'Aria* at the Museum für Gestaltung Zürich. Naturally that meant a lot to me as its editor. It was like receiving a personal Compasso d'Oro from a friend.

Then I Ran out of Breath

Verbal Doodling

The year was 1995 and we were at last ready: The first solo show devoted exclusively to Bruno Munari was about to open at the Museum für Gestaltung Zürich, exactly ten years after the ground-breaking *Ausdrucksformen—Achille Castiglioni, Designer* of 1985. Both exhibitions were installed in the main hall of the modernist building of 1933 designed by Steger and Egender, which incidentally is now a protected historical monument. Everyone came up from Milan for the opening: Dilma and Bruno, Jacqueline and Bruno, printers, publishers, collectors, fans, lenders, journalists, the designer Riccardo Blumer, and the architect Renato Stauffacher. One of my first invitees was Enzo Mari, as the option of doing his exhibition was still on the table. Mari had even received his invitation from me in person. When I called him to ask if I could reserve a hotel room for him he seemed standoffish at first, but accepted the offer. I then found him a room at a hotel nearby—not at Hotel Florhof, which is where the Munaris and Vodoz–Daneses were staying.

On the morning of the opening Mari called me at the studio. He was lucky to catch me at all,

Alfredo Häberli

as there was a press conference coming up at eleven and I was already on edge. I picked up the receiver with trepidation, only to hear that familiar voice booming out: "Qui Mari. Arrivo con il treno dopo le cinque. Stazione centrale di Zurigo. A dopo. Arriverderci Alfredo." I burst into tears! They were tears of joy, but also of relief as the pressure weighing on me subsided. The labels had not yet been mounted and there was still this and that to be done. But of course, I would have time for all that between the press conference and the opening at 7 p.m.—except that there was no question of anyone but me taking care of our guests. Those collectors of Munari's work had invited me over for dinner or coffee or taken me out to supper so many times, had showered me with such gifts, and had been so incredibly attentive to Stefanie, that I was determined to show them my appreciation in person. But with my co–curator Claude Lichtenstein busy writing his speech, a job he absolutely would not delegate, I was on my own.

On top of that Enzo Mari was arriving, meaning that he was already halfway to Zurich! Who would have thought it: Enzo Mari coming to the exhibition of his former friend and mentor Bruno Munari? Enzo Mari as the one who had brought Munari and Danese together in the first place? The train had arrived early—or perhaps I was late—and Mari was already walking towards me, even if he was too absorbed in sharpening his stick of licorice to look up at first. "È ancora in vita Munari?" he asked, once we had met. "Non è morto?" The callousness appalled me, and if that was his attempt at humor—well,to me it was not funny. "Signor Mari, la prego di non comunicare così, perché la lascio da solo qui per strada," I stammered. "Davvero! Non ce la faccio più!" I added for emphasis. Mari then softened and to placate me asked anxiously: "Alfredo, hai finito la mostra? E il libro?"

While Enzo and Bruno would greet each other later on, he ignored Dilma completely. Dilma, I think, had arrived at the same point as me. Sometimes you just have to take a step back. Otherwise it gets too much, becomes destructive, suffocating. Enzo knew Bruno's work, of course, but he took his time over the exhibition, and I gladly gave him that time. He liked my design of the display cases and the strip of spring steel on the floor that I had used to delimit the mobiles and the *Macchine inutile*. But on leafing through the catalogue he instantly discovered a mistake on page ninety-two: La libreria viaggiante Bompiani, a mobile bookstore dating from

Alfredo Häberli

1956, had been designed by him alone, he said. Munari had not been involved at all, which was indeed the case. Luckily for me that was the only mistake he found. Later, when we went to dinner at the Alpenrose within walking distance of the museum, I made sure to seat myself next to him, and thanks to this arrangement it turned out to be a genuinely harmonious gathering. Visits to restaurants with Dilma and Bruno were nothing new for me, but never before had I dined with Enzo, despite having repeatedly invited him to dinner at the Ristorante ai 3 Fratelli around the corner from his place.

The pressure was now off and I could relax. The content of the exhibition, the works and materials that I had selected, the design and style of the show, and the poster by Lars Müller, who also designed and published the book, garnered a lot of praise, including from many graphic designers and artists. The evening was a resounding success. Dilma, Jacqueline, Bruno, and Bruno then took a taxi back to Hotel Florhof and on bidding them goodnight I agreed to join them for breakfast next morning. Renato, Ricchi, Enzo, and I then went to the Kaufleuten–Bar for drinks. Stefanie drove us there in our trusty Fiat 128, just as she would later drive Enzo back to his hotel. What a picture that was: Enzo and Stefanie buzzing around

Zurich in a Fiat while we were hanging out at the bar! Next day, Riccardo Blumer gave Mari a ride back to Milan. Apparently, they got on just fine. "Che gran personaggio, il Mari," gushed Ricchi when he called me a little later. "Che grande! Veramente grande, non me l'aspettavo così forte!"

After the exhibition, I felt the urge to devote myself more to my own design work. As loyal as I would remain to the Museum für Gestaltung and its team of curators, and to exhibition-making generally for that matter, I was eager to get a foothold in the firms that I had set my heart on working for. I already had the necessary contacts in Italy, and slowly but surely the Italians were learning to say my name: "A–ber–li." The role of exhibition maker was a huge help in enabling me to approach the firms on my list, and knowing I had the Museum für Gestaltung behind me naturally boosted my confidence. The idea of staging an exhibition about Enzo Mari was still, as I said, on the table, although my role of co-curator would probably have to be redefined. Martin Heller, the director of the museum and a very good friend of mine, shared that view.

In the course of several meetings with Mari at his studio, we discussed his work at great length and through dialogue tried to fathom what design is all about. On one occasion, I was able to show him some of my own work, too—mostly student projects, but also some furniture prototypes, models from my internship, and exhibition designs. His verdict? I had some talent, for sure, but these were all lightweight things. I should do something more substantial, give weightiness a try, work with stone, perhaps, or some other solid material. He nevertheless looked carefully at each picture in turn, scrutinizing every one of them. And so we became friends—to the extent that Enzo Mari let anyone at all get close to him. We were on one of our many strolls along Corso Magenta one day when, on passing the Chiesa di Santa Maria delle Grazie, he suddenly said, "Alfredo, you just have to go and see Leonardo da Vinci's *Last Supper*," to which I replied, "Yes, I'll do that for sure, but I'd actually rather invite you for supper."

"Buonasera professore," said one of the three Fratellis standing in front of the restaurant of that name, as if on cue. But Mari cordially took his leave and disappeared into the apartment building where presumably Lea Vergine was waiting for him. That wonderful woman, an esteemed art critic in her own right, whom I knew only from the photos and postcards I had seen in Bruno Munari's archive, was Enzo Mari's life partner.

El hombre que me hizo observar el mundo: Enzo Mari

Verbal Doodling

"I am a great admirer of anonymous objects; of objects that have evolved over time; of artifacts that someone thought up as a solution to a very specific problem, inventing something simply because it did not yet exist. I am a great admirer of people who are constantly searching for truth, for honesty, and who are fearless about taking up challenges. I am a great admirer of people who manage to invest what they create with a soul, with beauty, with poetry that has no need of language, even though there is so much to say, so very much to say. I am an admirer of such people and am fortunate in having been able to watch them at work, to meet them more than once in the flesh, to get to know them personally, to receive help and guidance from them, to see and understand them. I am a great admirer of such people, and I had the great good fortune, the desire, and the time, to engage in depth with the complex, wide-ranging, and highly idiosyncratic oeuvre of one of them in particular: Enzo Mari. Added to which was the great good fortune of getting to know Enzo Mari personally.

Alfredo Häberli

"Hanging on the wall is a signed screen print of his *(Hammer and Sickle),* lined up on the rack are a number of his books (including some that Enzo Mari himself copied just for me), on the table is a copy of *Putrella,* stacked up in the display case are the *16 Animali,* standing on the sideboard is a marble vase, I myself am right now sitting on a *Box Chair* or a *Sof–Sof,* and I also possess fragments of his furniture as reference objects (a *Daniele* sofa, the leg of a *Filo di Ferro* table), as well as various dishes and (as a non–smoker) ashtrays. Lying on the *Thinking Man's Chair* before my very eyes, moreover, is *Domus* No. 607 of 1980.

"I am a great admirer of the work, the personality, the man Enzo Mari. Sometimes I had to step back from our many meetings and discussions because they affected me too deeply, because his observations of our world infuriated me. Enzo Mari asked me to look out of the window, to contemplate the world, the world of the Piazzale Baracca outside his studio, and to tell him how we are doing. *How are we doing?* I was lucky enough to see his exhibition in Milan, and even luckier to make Enzo Mari smile."

Arquitectura y Diseño, No. 233, February 2021

When I told Enzo of the birth of our first child, our son Luc, he asked me to call in at his studio next time I was in Milan. He had something for me, he said.

It was so wonderfully moving—all those gifts that Stefanie and I received from my customers at the births of our two children, Luc and Aline: an orange *Mezzadro* stool by Achille Castiglioni from Eleonora Zanotta and Daniele Greppi, who had taken over the technical department at Zanotta, an *Alvar Aalto* from Iittala—a flat vase with the child's name and date of birth engraved in it symbolizing the Finnish custom of "watering" the child from a baptism bowl—and a little bird by Oiva Toikka for Aline. But the most unusual gift of all came from Enzo Mari. It was intended not just for us parents, but also for our newborn Luc. "I know you don't understand politics and never will," said Enzo, with characteristic bluntness on presenting it to me, "and that's why I'm giving your son this serigraph, this screen print, so that you can hang it on the wall above his crib [he actually used the Italian word *cuna*, which has strong biblical associations], just to make sure he turns out well, and so he learns something about politics." I stood there dumbfounded, lost for words. That is how Enzo was. I doubt there are many design fans who ever received a gift from Enzo Mari on the birth of their child. That he wanted to give me something for our son, that he wanted it to be an unambiguous gesture—that I could understand. But a Hammer and Sickle above the cot? Yet there it was, *L'anniversario, Falce e martello,* signed, red on blue. I hid it on top of a cupboard in Luc's room and thought that one day, when he was older, I would hand it over to him, but I could not bring myself to hang it up on the wall right away. No, I could not do that to such an innocent little thing.

Luc, of course, has since grown up and, as promised, took possession of the signed screen print on his eighteenth birthday. He is now at university, studying History, Geography, and Political Science. So Enzo's prophecy came true.
And the print is at last hanging on Luc's wall.

Rolf Fehlbaum or How to Take Pleasure Seriously

Verbal Doodling

Long hair and a mustache, metal–rimmed glasses (though not by Max Bill), black suit and white shirt, unremarkable, unassuming, but acutely observant: that was the Rolf Fehlbaum I spotted in a gallery in Milan during the Salone one year—probably 1987, so on my second visit to the Milan furniture fair. I remember very clearly the pull–out table and bench combination, the *Tabula Rasa* by Ginbande—aka Uwe Fischer and Achim Heine—which Vitra would go on to produce in a limited edition; and there were designs by Coop Himmelb(l)au, Richard Artschwager, Ron Arad, Shiro Kuramata, Ettore Sottsass, Frank Gehry, and others, too. But the *Tabula Rasa,* I believe, was how Rolf first made his mark at Vitra. Feeling rather unsure of myself, given that I knew him only from photographs, I realized that I would have to simply bite the bullet and address him head on, that being the only way of finding things out in those pre–internet days. I was driven by my thirst for both knowledge and practical information, such as the address of a certain Japanese designer in Tokyo, for which I had to ask the right person.

Alfredo Häberli

Deciding that I had nothing to lose, I went up to the retiring, unassuming man described above, and said: "Excuse me, are you not Mr. Fehlbaum?" But when he responded in the affirmative, he said it so softly that I felt as if I had done something unseemly. "I'm a design student at the Schule für Gestaltung Zürich," I continued. "Forgive me for accosting you like this—" "That's all right," he interrupted reassuringly—"but I would very much like to do an internship with Shiro Kuramata and for that I need his address, which I thought you might have." "Yes, I do," he replied. "Shiro Kuramata is a very interesting person. Difficult to understand, but a very interesting person." He seemed to be pondering something. "I just gave a presentation on the history of design," I soldiered on, "precisely because there's so much that I don't understand, so much that is alien to me," I added. "Yes. Design is exciting," he said simply. So he was laconic, too, and as ponderous as ever. I began to wish I had not been so forward. I felt so ashamed, I wanted to sink into the floor. What effrontery—to barge in on a total stranger whom I knew only from photographs in a magazine! The Swiss are very protective of their privacy and what I was doing was simply not done. But I was young, and Argentinian, and I had long hair that I wore tied back in a ponytail.

"What's your name?" Rolf Fehlbaum asked. Was he trying to get rid of me or had I not offended him after all? "Alfredo Häberli." "And where do you live?" "In Zurich." I think I managed to mumble the district and the street, though nothing more than that. "Then I'll send you the address as soon as I can," he said. "Goodbye." So that was that, and all that I wanted now was to get out of there as fast as possible. It was all so embarrassing. Back out on the street I felt euphoric one moment and utterly mortified the next. But this was Milan, this was the place to meet people I knew only from pictures. And sometimes it wasn't even the people, but rather the products that I went off in search of. My curiosity knew no bounds. This was my world, my parallel world to design school. Milan was different, and what I saw there was different. What I had just seen in the gallery, for example, was unlike anything that I was learning in Zurich.

When I returned home two days later, I discovered that Rolf Fehlbaum's secretary had sent an envelope containing Kuramata's address in my mailbox. I could scarcely believe my eyes. How had he been able to remember my name without even noting it down? How had he found the right address?

At least now I had Kuramata's address and was a little closer to my goal. So now what? Among the Japanese books in the library of the Museum für Gestaltung was one about the Japanese tradition of wrapping things, called *How to Wrap Five More Eggs*. I thought that what I needed most was some special packaging for my request—perhaps a carefully crafted box containing four slides of my work and a letter folded lengthways addressed to Kuramata in hopes of his accepting me for an internship.

The question of how I would actually get to Tokyo or finance the internship had not yet occurred to me. All that mattered was that Kuramata's work fascinated me, especially that profiled in *The Architectural Review* No. 1089 "Japan." The magazines were a great way of finding out what was going on and were full of projects by all sorts of architects and designers. *The Architectural Review* No. 1074 "The New Spirit" springs to mind, for example, as does *L'Architecture d'Aujourd'hui* No. 237 "Technologiques" with works by Jan Kaplicky and Peter Rice, and a very fine portrait of Philippe Starck:

"Starck par lui–même:
— 35 ans.

— marié depuis 15 ans.
— vit dans l'avion.
— ne boit que du champagne et en boit trop.
— grand.
— gros.
— sale.
— mal élevé.
— très aimable.
— travaille seul avec sa femme.
— ne dort pas la nuit.
— a peu de théories.
— a très peu de temps…"

My one huge advantage was my easygoing, Latin character, my fearlessness about going off in search of happiness and following my heart's desire. I was also fortunate in having parents who had endowed their children with a strong sense of self-worth. We had lost everything and had had to leave everything behind in Argentina, so whatever came next was a gift. Our gift was our parents, who deliberately chose to work for Swissair if only to make visits to our grandparents, uncles, and other relations in Argentina more affordable. As family members, we were able to fly very cheaply—sometimes even for free.

This explains my habit of flying to cities that interested me as often as I could. I flew to Paris,

Alfredo Häberli

London, Madrid, Barcelona, and even Milan. Instead of going to discos at the weekend, I visited exhibitions, although I did sometimes go to those foreign discos that I had read about in the magazines: Otto–Zutz, KGB, Universal, Les Bains Douches, Café Costes, Parc de la Villetes, Institute Monde d'Arbe. Paris, London, Barcelona—I lapped them all up. And that was possible only because of our parents, who told us that wherever we wanted to go, they would pay the fare. After all, there is only so much that you can learn from books, and no one ever learned to live just by reading about it in a book.

The Friendship with RF, as We Called Him

Verbal Doodling

From time to time I would send Rolf Fehlbaum a postcard from here or there, and of course we ran into each other at trade fairs. Rolf also took to hosting a dinner party for Vitra designers during the furniture fair in Milan. It was an event for us alone, exclusively for designers with hardly any Vitra people there at all. Jasper Morrison, Antonio Citterio, Zaha Hadid, Alberto Meda, Hella Jongerius, and later Erwan and Ronan Bouroullec all came along, as did would-be Vitra designers like Konstantin Grcic and I.

By then I was on friendly terms with Rolf. We shared the same curiosity, the same respect for the task in hand. But what should I design? I was no Shiro Kuramata—who was so unlike anyone else. Nor was I a Maarten van Severen, who came to design from art, or an Alberto Meda, whose approach was more that of an engineer. My stance was closer to that of Morrison or Citterio, both of whom carried some weight at Vitra. Of course, I sometimes caught myself thinking: "That could have been by me" or "I could have done that too." But the real question was, why hadn't I? Even while a student at design school, I had understood that the complexity of an idea and its execution—actually making it, in other words—are not so easy to imitate. I had never believed in copying, because for me the focus was always on autonomy; or on that one tiny step that leads to a new idea. I saw that in my fellow designers and in their designs for Vitra, too; but I was not there yet.

Those Vitra dinners, like the Kvadrat dinners, were the most worthwhile evenings that I ever spent at the Salone del Mobile. Once I even missed picking up a design prize awarded me by a magazine, after reasoning with myself that spending time with my designer friends ultimately meant more to me, especially as not all of them were people I got to see between fairs. I talked regularly to Konstantin and Jasper on the phone, and Meda and I sometimes ran into each other at Alias or Luceplan, but I never saw Citterio.

There was always a kind of self–sorting into young and old at those dinner parties, and perhaps also into those who had made it and the young rebels. Once I was seated between Citterio and Meda and remember being impressed by the former's knowledge of finance, banking, and the stock market. It was more like sitting next to a stockbroker than an architect. But his work is impressive nonetheless. I would have loved to have designed the *Diesis* sofa (with Paolo Nava) for B&B, the drawer cabinets for Kartell, and *Spoon* for Iittala. This need is my way of awarding an Oscar to my design colleagues, though never without a twinge of constructive jealousy. Yes, I would have loved to design the *Diesis* sofa: the airiness of that cast aluminum frame with all that wonderful brass trim; those soft leather seat cushions and backrest and then the floppy armrests, lying so casually and unobtrusively on either side. It was a design coup—which of course is why the sofa has been in production for fifty years. Perhaps it is no longer selling quite so well, but it certainly shaped the early work of Citterio's collaboration with B&B. Then came *Sity, Charles,* and the others, and we got talking. Perhaps Citterio's interest in the stock market and investments was simply a consequence of all the royalties he had earned on the various sofas that he had designed over the years. I was somewhere else entirely, but happy and grateful to be present at those dinners. Afterwards we went to the Bar Basso, where the conversation turned to other matters—and not just the history of the bar, the Venetian goblets, the quality of the cocktails, or even the barkeepers, for that matter.

Those Vitra dinners were a fixture of the Salone for a number of years, though they eventually began to wear thin. The guests became noisier and nerves were increasingly on edge. Rolf himself wanted to change things and the furniture industry itself was in crisis.

"Can it be, Alfredo," asked Enzo Mari on the phone one day, "that the most important chair museum in Europe, perhaps even in the world, does not have a single chair by me in its collection?" He was referring to the Vitra Design Museum in Weil am Rhein, Frank Gehry's first building in Europe. "Of course not," I replied. "If I had a chair museum, it would definitely have an *Autoprogettazione,* a *Box Chair,* and a *Delfina.*" "And a *Tonietta,*" added Enzo for good measure. "Do you know anyone at Vitra?" he asked, knowing full well that I had known Rolf Fehlbaum since the 1980s.

I immediately called Rolf, and since I already knew his secretary, Helga Scheuring, was immediately put through to him. "RF" did not know exactly what the museum had in its collection, but he did know Enzo Mari and the four chairs that we had named. He promised to talk to Alexander von Vegesack, the museum director, and to get back to me once he had found out more. It was vintage Rolf: resolute, businesslike, short, and to the point.

It turned out that Enzo was right: The chair museum did not have a single chair by him, and Rolf, too, was of the opinion that it should. He therefore suggested that we meet at the next furniture fair in Milan and visit Enzo's studio together. He was interested only in the very first prototypes, he said, the older the better. The most important thing, however, was to meet and get to know Enzo in person.

That was something that I was good at: bringing people together—good people, that is, since what counted was of course the content. Enzo knew that, and Rolf, too, made full use of it. It is a gift that many company directors have—this ability to use their connections and their awareness of others to their own advantage. It was certainly one of Rolf's strengths, and it stood him in good stead right from the start.

But back to my story: I called Enzo, who true to character was begrudgingly pleased with the outcome of my efforts, though it still irked him that the museum itself had not come up with the idea of choosing one of his chairs for its collection.

Alfredo Häberli

Months later, after some hard drinking at the Bar Basso the night before, had it not been for Robert Wettstein waking me up, I would have overslept and missed the meeting with Rolf Fehlbaum at the Studio Enzo Mari that I had taken such pains to arrange. My role was simply to introduce them to each other and then to interpret for them, since Rolf spoke French, but no Italian, and Enzo spoke no English. Fortunately, the studio was just a short walk away from Hotel Speronari, so I arrived only a few minutes late. Rolf was already there, of course, and to my great surprise had the journalist Federica Zanco with him, whose articles for *Domus* I knew well. That meant that my services as an interpreter were no longer needed. I was cross with myself for having arrived late, as Enzo was already in full swing, showing his guests around his studio. Surprisingly, the real finds were in the bathroom, where a board placed on top of the bathtub had turned it into a pedestal for the first prototype of the *Box Chair* with fabric backrest; but there was also a *Delfina*, a *Sof–Sof,* and at the entrance his chair No. 1, the legendary *Autoprogettazione.*

Federica Zanco was wandering about on her own, peering at everything and only half listening. Like me, she wanted Rolf and Enzo to do the talking, which they were now doing in French—never mind that Enzo's theories and discourse only really work in Italian. When we gathered around his worktable an hour later, he unceremoniously plonked an *Eames* aluminum office chair on the table and, typically for him, launched into a critique of the design. Knowing that one of Charles and Ray Eames's maxims was "The details are not the details, the details make the product," and that the invisible underside of a product also matters, he examined the details carefully and asked Rolf why it had been made this way. This put both Rolf and me on the spot, though neither of us rose to the bait. Rolf made no attempt to defend the Eames chair, even if Enzo clearly wanted us to know that he considered its fame unwarranted.

Eventually, Rolf turned to Enzo and asked him what kind of chair he would make for Vitra. Enzo, who still craved recognition—monetary recognition—for his work, said that if he did anything at all, then only together with me. He thought highly of me, and the fact that I lived in Switzerland and spoke the vernacular—the German dialect we call Schwiizerdütsch—would make everything so much easier. His first task, he added, would be to improve this famous chair. Rolf judged that to be a good start and asked Enzo to get back to him so that he could show him (or rather us) the architectural highlights of the Vitra campus.

Months passed without any word from Enzo. I saw him several times during that period, but there was no mention of Vitra. Since I happened to have a meeting with Rolf one day, I asked him if he had heard from Enzo. No, he had not. So next time I saw Enzo, I reminded him that he was supposed to get in touch with Rolf, well knowing that he would never do so. For him it was up to the manufacturer to get in touch. Enzo was stubborn and bullheaded. Still more months elapsed. Yet Rolf had not asked much of him—just a call.

I had experienced something similar myself. If anyone other than me picked up the phone when Zanotta called, they would simply hang up. My assistants learned to tell me which song was playing at the other end of the line so that I would know who had called. If it was UB40, then the caller was Daniele Greppi from the technical department at Zanotta. The Italians always had their calls put through by their secretaries. I suspect because they feel less comfortable talking on the phone in a language that is not their own and where they have no recourse to gesticulation. Hence their propensity to hang up, or never to call at all. Another habit of theirs was to glance at their appointments' diary, discover a meeting scheduled for later that same day, and then call to confirm it, without realizing that in order to make it there on time I would have to be on the road by now. It is habits and peculiarities like these that over the years have enabled me to form a picture of many different nationalities.

Needless to say, Enzo never called, and Rolf never stopped waiting for him to call.

One day I received an inquiry about the possibility of working together with Fritz Hansen of Denmark. Since I did not want to work in parallel for two competitors on the same market and my dream had always been to work for Vitra, I decided to tell Rolf of my dream and the dilemma that I was now facing. He thought highly of Fritz Hansen, he said, but they could do with a really good designer. At Vitra, by contrast, it was like in Rome, where several deputies shared the same role. Vitra's furniture collection was the work of many hands, whereas a designer at Fritz Hansen would be like the mayor of a country town: alone, all–powerful.

Alfredo Häberli

But I could not bear to betray my dream. The impression made on me by that first encounter with Rolf in Milan, the first Vitra catalogue for its limited series of designs by Coop Himmelb(l)au, Shiro Kuramata, Ron Arad, and Ginbande, and even its advertising campaigns with such big names as Issey Miyake, Louise Bourgeois, and Billy Wilder all seated on a Vitra chair had been too profound for me to let it go. I saw all those designs as a gift from heaven, as salvation from the dogmas I had been force fed as a student. And there was another design world, too: the world of Milan.

"RF" asked me what I would like to design for Vitra, which was not an easy question. Whenever I am asked to create something for a new client, I always look for a niche, for a product typology that does not yet exist or has hitherto been neglected. That is why I began by defining an all–purpose chair that would be stackable and that could be lined up in long or short rows of seating—a task that I knew from the start would be difficult to accomplish. At the same time, I was also contemplating a desk chair for use in architects' offices, agencies, and perhaps even in the home. Here I was aiming for something with minimal movement, something less technical, modern, youthful, optically light, and visually appealing.

In the end we opted for the first idea. We spent two years working on the typology, on cardboard and later rigid–foam models, and on figuring out the plastics to be used, which we did in collaboration with Egon Bräuning and his team of Vitra's own engineers. It was a long–drawn–out process, and not at all easy, as the bar that Vitra had set was high— very high. But I was no longer daunted by such challenges, as I had enough experience under my belt by then.

And then came the day of the definitive go–ahead, after which the next step would be to invest in the necessary tools. On the drive from Zurich to Birsfelden—which is actually just 90 kilometers, though on that day it felt more like 300—I realized that the design was simply not good enough. We had tried to pack too much into that one idea. Sure, the chair had a certain charm, but no more than that. At the studio, I often ask my team: Would you want to buy it? It is a question that appeals directly to their innermost desires, to their gut feelings. Does it grab you? Does it speak to you? Does it move you? Answering those questions for myself, I knew that our design was not good enough; and only designs that I consider good enough are allowed to leave my studio. This freedom is a luxury that I have had the privilege of being able to insist on ever since my apprenticeship—especially since having my own studio. There can be no compromise on matters of the heart, at least not for an artist or a designer.

So those were the thoughts going through my head on the drive to Vitra with my assistant in the passenger seat. I kept them to myself, however, communing only with my Saab 900 Turbo Cabriolet. It was to be a large meeting with nearly a dozen people at the table, including Egon Bräuning. He was extremely important to Rolf, as he always listened carefully and was a good judge of whether an idea was practicable. I got on very well with Egon, but he was not always popular with us designers, as not every idea got past him. Egon might declare an idea unfeasible, which is something no designer likes to hear. There were other engineers and draftsmen at the table as well as some people from marketing and design, and, of course, Rolf himself, who is always present when a design is on the line. He has this gift of asking questions thatpinpoint the critical issues with surgical precision. If Rolf asks something, you know that it matters. His reflections are always sound and very exact.

The meeting began with coffee and small talk to put everyone at their ease, but then the moment had come and I knew that I had to get in there first before any official decision was made. "I know that what I'm about to say will be disappointing and disquieting," I began, "and I definitely share that unease, but I have the feeling that there is something not quite right about this design. I know how expensive the tools for it will be, and I also know how much time and effort we have all invested in it, but I, personally, would not buy this chair."

There, I had said it. My assistant was astounded, as were the engineers—in fact, everyone present in the Frank Gehry building in Birsfelden that day was. It was like standing at the altar of a church and saying "No." "That's the end of my friendship with Rolf," I thought glumly. The engineers tried to remonstrate with me—"We've come so far!"—but Rolf was having none of it: "Alfredo," he said. "I felt something similar, so I'm grateful for your candor." He then ended the meeting and dismissed everybody else so that we were the only two people remaining. "You know that's exactly what I appreciate about you," he mused. "Any other designer would have tried to sell his idea, would have tried to talk us into it, to win us over. But you speak from your guts. And because such things are incredibly hard to say, you just blurt it out." Then he, too, fell silent. "So what kind of project are we going to do now?" he asked. "I don't know, Rolf," I answered. "You may not want to work with me ever again. I'm really sorry, but it was only on the way here that is became so crystal clear to me." "Well never mind," said Rolf. My assistant and I then drove back to Zurich without exchanging a word.

A few months later, the half–produced tool along with all the models and prototypes for the ill–fated chair were exhibited alongside many other works of mine at the Museum für Gestaltung Zürich. That was the show *Alfredo Häberli Design Development, SurroundThings* (2008), my first monographic exhibition. The point of including them was to lift the lid on those processes and aspects of design work that are not so well known and that the failed project for Vitra exemplified very well.

Having thus unburdened myself, the next idea was not long coming: I was going to design a plywood chair, since the only other plywood chairs in the Vitra catalogue were the *DCM* by Ray and Charles Eames and a design called *Taino* that made no sense to me. I called

Rolf right away. He thought it an interesting idea and instantly gave me the go-ahead.

Jill went on the market three years later, in 2011. It is made using a patented procedure that entails cutting the shell out of a single piece of flat plywood, bending it into shape, and then connecting the seat down the middle to give it its sculptural form. Ray and Charles Eames had conducted endless experiments with plywood in the 1950s, and had switched to plastic only after failing to achieve a plywood chair of satisfactory quality. That, however, is another story and a well-documented chapter of design history.

Verbal Doodling

Martin Heller or: What Are You Working On?

I had just begun my design course at the Schule für Gestaltung when I went to see Martin Heller, who had recently been appointed curator of the Museum für Gestaltung Zürich. He was surprised to see someone from the design school affiliated to his museum, but also pleased, given that I had come to ask for a job to help me through college. He asked me what I could do and what I had in mind, so I told him that I could draw—well he could do that, too, he said—and that I had done an apprenticeship as an architectural draftsman and was good with my hands. I also knew how to work the school's fleet of machines, which was stretching the truth somewhat, as I had only just begun to get the hang of them.

A few weeks later, Martin came to visit me at the interior architecture and design studio and told me that he perhaps had a job for me. Would I be up to "making" an exhibition, he asked? The reason he said "making" so emphatically, he added, was that the work would fall during the summer vacation, meaning that there would be no handymen around to help me. That, then, was the start of a collaboration and friendship that would last for many years. I had found not only a job, but also a mentor who was to have a tremendous impact on my development and to whom I owe a great deal.

When I showed him my first sketches, Martin listened carefully to what I was saying and then asked: "Alfredo, what are you working on? What is it about? Try summarizing your idea in a single sentence!" This method influenced me just as much as the probing and contemplation of a theme from different perspectives, yet I learned it not from school but from my client, mentor, and friend Martin Heller. It was also from him that I learned that content counts and is actually all that counts, even if that means a leap of faith on the part of the designer. Anxious to make the exhibition as good as possible, Martin also called in some specialists, who were not necessarily his best friends.

He got the most out of us youngsters—out of everyone in fact—by setting very high standards. He nurtured us, but also made demands of us; and as someone who promoted innovation and who knew himself well, he could be at once diplomatic and provocative. He

Alfredo Häberli

was also eloquent ("What is it about?"), a conceptual genius ("How does it work?"), and a master of getting straight to the point ("What are you working on?"). The titles and content of his exhibitions read like manifestos penned in his own hand. For all of that I am deeply grateful to him.

Martin Heller was only indirectly connected to Milan, but he still had a formative impact on my career, because the work I did for him was "visible" work that I could then show to others. He was also among those who supported my idea of staging exhibitions on Enzo Mari and Bruno Munari at the Museum für Gestaltung.

His premature death in October 2021 just three days before his sixty–ninth birthday upset me deeply. His promise to write the foreword of my next book will forever haunt me.

Riccardo Sarfatti, a Beacon of Light

Verbal Doodling

On my many trips to Italy, and to Milan especially, I had developed the almost manic habit of buying as many design magazines as I could lay my hands on; not because they cost only a third of what they cost in Switzerland, but because the design press in Italy was quite different. The periodicals I bought in Milan, Barcelona, London, or Paris were just as crucial to my research as were my visits to the library of the Schule für Gestaltung or Zurich's central library. This was how information was circulated in the modern world. I was interested mainly in cartoons, art, architecture, and design, and later in fashion, too. I still possess those magazines, even today: *The Architectural Review* and later *Blueprint* from England, *Madriz* (200 pesetas, 1986), *Ardi, De Diseño,* and later *On* from Spain, *L'Architecture d'Aujourd'hui* and *Intramouros* from France, and *Abitare, Ottagono* (the first one hundred issues were fabulous!), *Rassegna* (thematic), and above all *Domus* (for just 3,000 lire!) from Italy. For me they are like books, and every time I leaf through them I discover something new. They were my "source of life and dreams," and one of those dreams was to one day open such a magazine and discover an article all about me and my work. If only I could get that far! They were my reference library, my compass, and the very antithesis of what I was doing at design school all rolled into one. They helped me sort out who I was and what I wanted.

The architects' office where I did my apprenticeship subscribed to *werk, bauen + wohnen* and *Archithese*. Sometimes I also bought the German art magazine *Art*—at least when the group known as the "Neue Wilden" were all the rage. And when I had a girlfriend in Ticino, she gave me the same wonderful gift month after month: a copy of the latest *Domus* with her own sweet messages to me scribbled into the ads. Those, too, I have archived. As a student in New York and San Francisco I discovered still more periodicals: *Emigre* from California and *Pamphlets* by Storefront, an architecture gallery just below SoHo in New York City.

Many years later, by which time I had almost forgotten that dream of mine, *Domus* No. 760 of 1994 (which by then cost 15,000 lire) published an article about my work running to several pages; *Abitare* No. 338 followed suit in 1995, as would *Interni, Intramuros, Design Report,* and others. One day, after the publication of a piece about my work as an exhibition architect in *Abitare*, I received a call: "Pronto? pronto? qui Paolo Rizzatto! Con chi parlo? Pronto?!" There was evidently an Italian on the line and it turned out to be Paolo Rizzatto, designer of the *Costanza* lamp. I was lost for words and felt as if I were floating five centimeters off the floor. "Pronto!"—Rizzatto was getting impatient, which is typical of Italians on the phone, as I later came to appreciate.

Rizzatto was summonsing me to a meeting in Milan with him and Riccardo Sarfatti, CEO of Luceplan, though whether it was at Ernesto Teodoro Moneta's address I cannot say. This was the mid–1990s, around the time of the Bruno Munari exhibition. Rizzatto, who was a friend and neighbor of Italo Lupi, wanted to introduce me as a young designer and to give me a theme to work on. He seemed to think that I was an expert in exhibitions, including touring exhibitions—hence his reference to the show *Gebrauchsanweisung* of 1992, which had visited Zurich, Amsterdam, and New York. My task was to devise a kind of art display or three–dimensional catalogue so that Luceplan could exhibit its complete range of lamps in as small a space as possible. Two different versions were needed: one for lamps for the home and another for technical lighting fixtures for mounting on the wall or incorporating into other installations. It certainly made sense, as retailers often lack the space to display their wares properly.

When it came to the tricky matter of my fee, I was introduced to Sarfatti, a very elegant, good-looking gentleman, as cultured as he was courteous. He asked me what I was going to charge, and there it was, my second Milanese nightmare after the experience with my sister's Golf and our first night at the Hotel Speronari. I needed time to think it over, I stammered, but then decided to play for high stakes. I began by telling him of my dream of one day becoming a designer, and of one day designing a lamp and not just exhibitions, and that I was already in talks with Flos, which was not actually true, but rather my inner Argentinian taking over. Exhibitions were an interesting "training ground," I continued, and they had certainly helped me to pay my way through college, but I had no wish to be pigeonholed as an expert exhibition-maker.

"Ho capito bene," said Sarfatti, who had known nothing of all this, but understood me right away. He promised me that I would be considered as a potential young designer of lamps for Luceplan, and he assured me that he was the one who made such decisions, which was definitely good to hear. But the matter of my fee was still unresolved. Then it flashed through my head: Why not just ask for what I had received from the Museum für Gestaltung? The trouble was, I first had to convert it into lire and when I did that I got it wrong by a factor of ten! Lire prices always came with a long string of naughts behind them, so the figure I quoted did not seem too exorbitant. "That's a lot," said Sarfatti. "I know you have a studio in Switzerland and that labor costs there are higher than here, but that's a whole year's salary for one of our office staff." My heart was thumping like crazy; after all, the project would take me at least half a year, and I, too, had rent and taxes to pay. "We'll pay you half that," said Sarfatti, "and for that you can draw me a lamp for Luceplan."

I had miscalculated my fee and Riccardo Sarfatti had met me half way! What an incredible stroke of luck! Thanks to my gambling high and getting the sums wrong I was now going to be paid five times what the museum had paid me! Sarfatti and I shook hands. It was a deal. One curious aspect of my personality that

Alfredo Häberli

I inherited from my father and cherish to this day is my belief in the value of a gentleman's agreement. Any lawyer, any manager would caution against it, but that's just how I work. For me, a gentleman's word really is his bond, and although I have suffered the occasional breach of trust in the thirty-year history of my studio, I choose to remain incorrigibly old-fashioned on this point. If you shake on it, it's a deal. This is also one of the reasons why I have no time for people who never take risks, who do only what they are told, who never go out on a limb. Hence that poster of mine from a few years back that said: "Say what is. Do what you say. And be what you do."

Saying nothing is also a stance, of course, though to me, saying nothing means not taking a stand. The manifesto was my response to what was happening in the furniture industry, the design scene, and to management and industry generally at the time. The collections were beginning to look more and more alike, and risks were being minimized so that if a product was doing well, the next one would look much the same.

The project for Luceplan was a success. We produced two displays: a thousand of one and five hundred of the other. Since it had to be affordable, we looked for a low–cost material to work with and found it in oriented strand board or OSB, a kind of coarse fiberboard. Each display consisted of two boards of 100 × 200 centimeters and was shipped as a flatpack, although making it three–dimensional was easy enough. The name we chose for it, *Pop–Up,* says it all. We had developed a two–way hinge for it and had had an aluminum molding made specially for that purpose. What we had not taken into account, however, was the time it took to mount those hinges; because although each hinge required only two screws, in practice this meant an assembly time of two months. Yet I knew from Enzo Mari that labor costs were the highest they had ever been. For him it had been an issue with projects such as his *Autoprogettazione* and even the *Java* sugar bowl (1968) for Danese; yet the importance of not having to screw on a hinge by hand, of a design intelligent enough to obviate that extra step—we had completely lost sight of that. Knowing the labor–hours needed for assembly was actually extremely important.

At least we developed the minimal transport packaging and wordless assembly instructions ourselves. The magazines were happy to publicize the work, too, and we even staged a little exhibition at the pavilion on the Luceplan premises. Paolo Rizzatto and even Sandra Severi Sarfatti, who was in charge of graphic design and communications, were also involved, and the friendship that developed between us has endured to this day. One perk of the job was the unforgettable experience of unpacking each of the Luceplan lamps in turn, which gave me a chance to analyze them closely. That is exactly what I mean by my own aphorism: "Observation is the most beautiful form of thinking." Analyzing these products—the wonderful work of the lamp itself, the intelligent packaging, the style of the mount, the assembly instructions—taught me things that no book could have taught me, because these are things that have to be observed and absorbed. The fact that Luceplan's founding members were all architects was a tremendous asset and put it in a class of its own.

I found in Riccardo Sarfatti a *gran signore imprenditore,* a true entrepreneur and someone to look up to as a man of exquisite taste, a shrewd judge of design, and an eloquent orator in Italian. I also spent time with him in a private capacity. One of our most enjoyable moments was at his home in Milan, where we watched a soccer match together on TV. Both professionally and in private, he was always a true gentleman.

Many years later I told him the anecdote about how I had miscalculated my fee. It turned out that he had known it even at the time, but had regarded the high price as an investment in something and somebody he believed in. Then he said that perhaps I could do him a favor in return. He had a Rolex *Air–King* with a dark–blue dial that he had inherited from his father, Gino Sarfatti, and wanted me to take it to Rolex in Switzerland for servicing. At Rolex they told me the story of this special watch and how it had once made the journey to Venice via Athens. They knew this because every time a Rolex is opened, the horologist makes a tiny engraving in the watchcase. Gino Sarfatti had also been a *gran signore produttore,* an inspired designer of lamps and the founder of Arteluce.

Today I often wonder what we ourselves inherit and then pass on to our children in our genes, in our blood. I know Gino Sarfatti only from books and above all from his lamp designs. He was probably the most gifted lamp designer of his time, but also one of the great producers in the history of design. The lamps of the Castiglioni brothers belong in the same illustrious sphere. But as an *imprenditore,* Sarfatti was unique, the kind of man that is almost never encountered these days. Perhaps there are simply far too many managers today, most of whom studied business and learned what they know from books, rather than on the job, or perhaps it is because they are not entrepreneurs and have never had to put their own money on the line. The difference is certainly striking, today more than ever.

Riccardo had undoubtedly inherited his father's courage, his readiness to take risks, his vision, his eye for the uniqueness of an idea, his reliance on his intuition and ability to act on it intelligently. Being able to put this into words was also a gift. "We must work in all directions at once and find at least something innovative in each of them," he once said. How else could projects such as *Costanza, Lola, Titania, Berenice, On Off, Fortebraccio* have come about? They were all such innovative, audacious designs, both materially and technically, and always on the verge of the feasible. Of course, the other co–founders of Luceplan, the designers (architects and engineers) Paolo Rizzatto and Alberto Meda, were also important. But the real driving force was Riccardo Sarfatti.

After the *Pop–Up* display, we developed the indirect lamp *Carrara,* the spray–painting of whose man–sized column called for one of the largest tools we had ever had to make. Then came *Lane,* a simple series of wall lamps, and *Sky,* a waterproof outdoor lamp that shines brightly and is powered solely by solar cells. But for me as an external designer to be showing off my work to a team of architects, engineers, and entrepreneurs who had design aspirations of their own was not such a great strategy, and before long I was "back in Rome," as Rolf Fehlbaum would have said.

I saw less and less of Sarfatti after he went into politics, gradually stepping back from Luceplan and letting other family members take over. His tragic death still upsets me. But I still develop lamps for his son, Alessandro Sarfatti, whom I have known since his youth, and who now runs A–Step, a design firm of his own in Copenhagen.

Verbal Doodling

Renato Stauffacher or Little, Tiny Sparks of Joy

In Switzerland, the date of December 6 is called "Samichlaus," which is the dialect name for the feast day of Saint Nicholas, who traditionally brings gifts for children. Over the centuries, however, the altruistic, benevolent bringer of bounty has morphed into a censorious tutor, even if the actual meting out of punishments is left to his sidekick "Schmutzli" (also known as Knecht Ruprecht). "Schmutzli" is the one who swings the cane, who scolds the disobedient, who threatens to tie naughty children up in a sack.

But adults also gather on this day, which is why Beat Cahenzli, Swiss agent of Alias, chose December 6 to invite the Alias CEO along with some customers to our spacious, light-flooded, two-story studio. This was my second studio, the one I shared first with Christophe Marchand and later with Robert Wettstein.

What had given Beat the idea was an article in *Hochparterre*—a periodical that specializes in architecture, planning, and design—illustrated with photographs of the former gallery that now served us as a studio. Since I had previously written to Alias, that is to say to its CEO Renato Stauffacher, an architect from Lugano and personal friend of Mario Botta, to express an interest in working for them, I was distraught at being unable to attend the planned meeting; I had previously arranged a trip to Argentina at exactly the same time and my flights could no longer be changed. It was like being punished by "Schmutzli" all over again!

Renato, however, made it clear that our correspondence would continue, and that loyalty has endured to this day. In fact, it is what characterizes both him as a person and our relationship. The pin–boards in the studio, the objects, the books, and the material research we were doing so impressed Renato that he did indeed consider working with me. All he had to do was await my return. On one of my many trips to Italy in search of interesting material for the Bruno Munari exhibition and to visit collectors of his work, I decided that since I was driving from Bolzano to Bergamo I might as well pay my first visit to Alias in Grumello del Monte and meet Renato in person. I arrived in the bright–blue Fiat 128 that Stefanie and

Alfredo Häberli

I had inherited from her great–aunt with nothing more than a cardboard box full of stuff and a few slides of my work. It was an exciting encounter from start to finish: exciting, candid, and direct. To get to know each other better, we decided to work on a tea trolley, a *complemento d'arredo* as the Italians so fittingly call such items, and the kind of thing that Achille Castiglioni and Vico Magistretti excelled in. If done properly, such accessories can really shine, can become tiny sparks of joy. That first meeting with Renato was in the mid–1990s and marked the beginning of a long friendship.

The tea trolley project gave rise to a concept consisting of two H–sections with asymmetrical crossbars, meaning that they could be rotated through 180 degrees to produce different heights. Over the next two years, these cast aluminum H–sections gave rise to the *SEC* system unveiled at the 1997 furniture fair in Milan. *SEC* stood for "Systema Elementare Componibile," but also for "Systema Emozionale Componibile." It is a self–supporting aluminum frame that can be extended as required both vertically and horizontally and that is fitted with panels, shelves, drawers, and even doors. The panels were prints that could be made of a range of transparent, perforated, and matte materials. Put simply, they were elemental, emotionally charged surfaces—hence the name.

Like so many of the encounters that I had in my early years, this one, too, would result in close collaboration. What made it so fruitful and distinctive was the ongoing dialogue with both the proprietors and the designers—all those hours we spent poring over sketches, appraising prototypes, and of course having lunch or dinner together. Since the project managers and marketing specialists took over, that kind of personal involvement is becoming ever rarer.

Yet it is precisely this friction, this confrontation, this critical engagement that gives true depth to a friendship, even if a shared interest in good food, architecture, art, and automobiles also helps. As CEO, Renato was remarkable for daring to do things differently, for being willing to work on visions, to follow his intuition, to take risks, to seek innovation, to tease out originality, to integrate intelligence, and to put his intellect to good use. Presumably this was also the path that he, as an outsider, had had to take; he had had to prove himself through his ideas, through his products. After all, there is very little money for sales and marketing in small firms such as Alias, which was never part of the Milanese establishment. Renato came from Brianza, which is famed for its hardworking craftsmen who work their magic in the innumerable small businesses based there. Industrious, highly skilled people like this are to be found all over northern Italy, even as far as Udine and Venice, and should definitely not be underestimated. They may be "little people," but they are a force to be reckoned with.

This appreciation of quality, and all the aforementioned character traits and idiosyncrasies, are what make up a truly *gran imprenditore;* and they are rare. Yet I was fortunate enough to meet some of them right at the start of my career, and so was able to internalize their values both as a designer and as a human being.

SEC won great acclaim on the market. It was clearly an anticyclical approach to the bending and welding of metal tubes, and Alias invested heavily in innumerable tools for this naturally photogenic, colorful, and contemporary product. The costs were horrendous, the materials heterogeneous, and the possible combinations and applications limitless—which made it all but inconceivable for a small Italian firm.

But it was Renato Stauffacher's Swiss side that sparked his fascination with a whole system and that drove us into the madness of a project that was to prove most instructive for my future career. Very few designers have this ability to think in systems and in this degree of complexity. So as painful as this phase was for me as a young designer, it was also an experience from which I learned a great deal.

My friendship with Renato and our mutual respect intensified over the years and we began to meet privately, too—in winter at Sils Maria or Ftan, or at Hotel Castell in Zuoz, where we would tour the local galleries together before or after lunch. We also met at the Villa d'Este on the Concorso d'Eleganza in Como, and Renato and his wife Barbara attended both the inauguration of my last but one studio and my fiftieth birthday party, which, thanks to the generosity of BMW Switzerland, I was able to celebrate among the "Art Cars"—that is, in the hall where the cars by Alexander Calder, Andy Warhol, Roy Lichtenstein, Jenny Holzer, and Jeff Koons are kept. That was also the venue for my receipt of the Swiss Grand Prix of Design awarded by the Swiss Federal Office of Culture, which had likewise had the idea of throwing a party in a glorified "parking lot!" Renato attended that event with his old friend Riccardo Blumer, who became a friend of mine, too.

Beat and Renato organized several excursions with us Alias designers. We visited works of architecture in Basel, Bern, Lucerne, and Zurich, as well as Peter Zumthor's Therme Vals, where we had the pleasure of seeing Alberto Meda, Paolo Rizzatto, and Riccardo Blumer in swimming trunks! Wining and dining were naturally an essential part of these trips. We also got into the habit of exchanging gifts—books, objects, pens, and such like, my last gift having been my own limited edition *Fixpencil* for Caran d'Ache, a variant of the original Swiss design of 1929. The many lunches we had together at the Osteria della Villetta in Palazzolo sull'Oglio were among our most creative moments. As an architect, Renato was in the habit of doodling on his table mat, which tellingly he did with a *Fixpencil*. We drew our concepts for the future, but were working very much in the here and now. Another recurring question was which products, which designs, we would take with us on our hypothetical Noah's Ark—a game which became our personal Compasso d'Oro for the designs we loved best.

Our selection alone would have been enough to fill a whole museum! And luckily for us, we were unencumbered by the conflicts and obligations that had dogged the real Compasso d'Oro since its inception in Milan in 1954. We were at liberty to admit or exclude whomsoever we wanted, nor did we need connections or have to repay past favors. The adjudication of our very own *Premio dell'Arca di Noè*, in other words, was genuinely independent. Either a design was on board, or, after further scrutiny, it was deemed not to merit a place among the chosen. Just how few designs made it onto the ark was astonishing, and our own creations were generally not among them. Being self–critical was important to us as both a motivation and a determination to do better.

That our powers of discrimination were constantly being honed by the exquisite Lombard cuisine on which Grazia and Maurizio Rossi lavished such love and care, not to mention the locally grown Franciacorta wines, goes without saying. The walls of the Osteria della Villetta are full of sketches, paintings, and bon mots by the many artists, architects, and designers who have dined at that wonderful temple to slow food. Good ideas take time, as does good food.

I have done around a dozen projects for Alias over the past twenty-five years: after *SEC* and *Legnoletto,* there was my first industrially made chair *Segesta,* the sofa *TT,* and then *Plein Air, Stabiles, Ago,* and so forth. Another research project was *Time,* an armchair whose shell is made of ultra-thin sandwich board just 2.5 millimeters thick, which is folded in three dimensions and then mounted on a steel frame. The designs for Renato were all distinctive, as is our friendship. Our loyalty to each other is certainly unusual, at least now that we live in an age of rapid turnover of both staff and management.

Our collaboration had a formative impact on much of my work as a designer. I mention this because there was something that Renato did that consistently led to heated but ultimately constructive discussions: He requested, or rather demanded, unconditional loyalty and devotion to Alias. Whatever furniture we produced was to be exclusively for Alias. Now that might be appropriate for architects, engineers, or artists— but designers?

Here, too, my role model was Achille Castiglioni, and I was constantly thinking how nice it must be to compartmentalize as he did, designing lamps for Flos, table objects for Alessi, furniture accessories for Zanotta, trade fair booths for Cassina and RAI, to say nothing of his various sofas and armchairs. Such clear–cut divisions between manufacturers—that was my dream, too; hence the importance of not being greedy and trying to design everything for everyone.

I saw my fellow designers create three different versions of the same design for three different manufacturers. To express it in allegorical terms, the Milanese design scene of the past ten years has become rather like the Three Musketeers from the 1844 novel of that name by Alexandre Dumas: Therein, the young hotspur d'Artagnan makes the acquaintance of two more–experienced, albeit reckless, musketeers, and together with them forms an elite fighting force, whose motto "one for all, all for one" might just as well apply to all those architects and designers of renown who do design work for one and all. Even if in this allegory d'Artagnan is female.

But such "promiscuity" was as inconceivable for me as it was for the great entrepreneurs of that time, and on this point, Renato and I were absolutely of the same mind. That my interest as a designer was not confined to the furniture industry was also a great asset. Like Achille, I also created electronic appliances, did studies for the automotive industry, and built works of architecture, so I had several strings to my bow and that enabled me to gain a wealth of experience.

Renato Stauffacher understood this—
and understood the value of it.

Riccardo Blumer and the Deceptive Lightness of Inquiry

Verbal Doodling

Friends of friends. Attending trade fairs and all the dinner parties and other social functions that such events entail enabled me to meet people I had not known previously. The encounters often took place backstage—that is, in the rear part of the booths where there was more privacy. Renato, however, found that setting insufficiently "communicative," since the point was not to hide or to exclude anyone, but rather just to sniff each other out. They were opportunities to make new acquaintances nonetheless—as with Giandomenico Belotti or Riccardo Blumer, an Italo–Swiss architect perhaps best described as an exploratory or investigative architect, or at any rate as one whose primary concern is not with commercial projects. Riccardo, who like Renato is also a friend of Mario Botta, is not only extremely gifted and highly intelligent, but he has an exceptionally lucid and subtle sense of humor, even if it only really works in Italian.

That is just one side of his character, however—one that is not apparent in his investigative projects. He is also someone who can doggedly pursue the same vision for years at a time, doing all the necessary experiments and developing all his own tests. For example, he had always wanted to develop a lightweight chair along the lines of Marco Zanuso and Richard Sapper's sheet-metal *Lambda,* and in pursuit of that goal had tried first a lightweight wooden frame, then balsa wood, then a wooden frame with foam infill—always keeping Renato in the picture, of course—until one day his *Laleggera* chair was ready to go into production. As a manufacturer, Renato saw this basic research work as the responsibility of the designer. He expected us to work on projects without any immediate commercial expectations, simply on the off chance that one of them might one day yield results. That, in fact, was one of Alias's great strengths, which is why the designs of Giandomenico Belotti, Mario Botta, Carlo Forcolini, and Alberto Meda were such an excellent fit. Its catalogue was on a similar scale to that of Zanotta, which Renato admired just as much as I did.

Riccardo saw only a few creations of his through to serial production, however, because what really interested him was the inquiry itself. Today he is Mario Botta's successor as director of the Accademia di architettura di Mendrisio, where he and his students are still engaged in research work.

Much the same thing happened with the *Spaghetti, Seconda, Frame, Apocalypse Now,* and *Ran* chairs, which made both Alias and their designers famous overnight, as did Riccardo with his wicked sense of humor and above all the research he did for *Laleggera*. He is one of a kind in the very best sense.

It was this same attitude, this same spirit of inquiry and the quest for new materials and manufacturing techniques—the Italian method, whose origins can be traced back to the Cassina & Busnelli products of the late 1960s—that made Italy world famous as the Land of Design. And the first design by Gaetano Pesce, his *Up* for Cassina & Busnelli, made that young architect world famous, too.

Verbal Doodling

Enrico Astori, at First a Fleeting Encounter

Enrico Astori and I first met in the 1980s at the Driade stand in Milan, where I introduced myself as a young student born in Argentina. I mentioned this knowing that all Italians have friends and family somewhere in Argentina. It was my standard opening gambit. Meeting people in person was always important, but how, after several failed attempts, I finally managed to accost Enrico, who seemed always to be otherwise engaged, remains a mystery to me.

To my great surprise, it turned out that not only did he have friends and family in Argentina, but he and his family had actually lived there for several years. And the second surprise was that he spoke Spanish, or at least understood it. He then showered me with all sorts of brochures topped by his personal calling card. The name ENRICO ASTORI was printed in capitals in the center, while the address at the bottom left was all lower case: via dei chiostri 1, milano tel. 872677. I still have that card. It was small, perhaps just 2×5 centimeters, and minimalist; and most important of all, it had class. To me it was worth more than my disco membership, my bank card, my annual pass to the Kunsthaus, and even my student ID. So strong was its allure—as is my memory of that first exchange with Enrico. Back home I told my father about it. The name Astori was familiar to him from the big construction company that prefabricated concrete sections for highways back in Argentina. Enrico Astori, Chairman of Driade, was apparently a scion of that same family.

I saw many exciting furniture designs on display at the Driade stand, including some by Philippe Starck *(Tippy Jackson)* and later Toyo Ito *(Uki Suki)*, Enzo Mari *(Frate)*, Antonia Astori *(Oikos)*, and Elliott Littman *(Betsy)*. So a visit to Driade was always on my itinerary whenever I was In Milan, whether at the Driade showroom on Via Fatebenefratelli and later Via Manzoni, or at the Salone. Enrico's calling card invariably served me as a kind of admission ticket, and he himself was always very courteous, welcoming me into his realm as a student and then as a young designer. I was full of respect for him, and a little fearful, because I thought he might have a weakness for young men. He always pointed out how beautiful my hair was, becaue I wore a long ponytail at the time. Was that the right look for a would–be designer? Many years would pass before I no longer cared about such things.

Alfredo Häberli

My lucky break came when Driade decided to develop two collections specially for young people, which after all those years of waiting, holding on, and trying over and over again, I was to develop together with Konstantin Grcic and Sebastian Bergne. The collections, to which I contributed two items of furniture and several small objects, were called *Atlantide* and *D.House,* and both were launched in 1997. Another one involved in their creation was Marco Romanelli, an architect–designer who as a journalist wrote the first article about my work for *Domus*. Over the years, all these individual encounters coalesced into a dense network of clients and fellow designers. Such networks take time to develop—and even more so, patience.

Enrico, like his wife Adelaide Acerbi, who was responsible for the graphic design and communications, was always very generous with his time. He was so incredibly knowledgeable and such a cultured man. His roots were in the Milanese haute bourgeoisie and he cherished them and celebrated them—at times unabashedly, at times more modestly. He kept open house at his home on Via dei Chiostri and hosted many an opulent dinner party there. Enrico took me under his wing in an almost paternal way and gave me his take on young designers. Only at the age of forty was anyone mature enough to become a designer, he once said, and on another occasion he lamented our tendency to repeat ourselves. Yet he also opened my eyes to the way periodicals and magazine articles work: If I booked the back cover of a magazine for several months running, he explained, then naturally I could expect a certain number of column–inches of copy in return. One purpose of the dinners to which I was frequently invited, he said, was to give journalists a chance to meet the newcomers on the scene, which meant people like me. While some of these insights were revelatory, others robbed me of my innocence. Suddenly, I lost all interest in the articles being published about me and for many years greeted them with indifference. While critique was very much an integral part of art and architecture, there was no such culture in design. On the contrary, the design industry seemed to live on a diet of constant praise and quid pro quos. Articles were financed indirectly, as were the various design prizes, even though what mattered most was to be self–critical—and to have the "right" friends.

I was a regular guest at the Astoris while preparing the Bruno Munari exhibition. They included me in their family lunches held every Wednesday, at which Adelaide Acerbi, the Astoris' daughters Elena and Elisa, and Enrico's sister Antonia were also present, along with various other guests. What a beautiful tradition that was! These events were not sumptuous, but the food was always excellent and the family chitchat engaging. It was on one such occasion that Adelaide told me that she had written her doctoral dissertation on Enzo Mari. She even fetched her Enzo Mari archive and gave it to me, clearly delighted to find a young designer who was just as enthusiastic about his work as she had been as a student. She was also pleased with herself for having discovered him first. She knew his work very well and she was the one who had brought him to Driade in person. Enrico had sometimes found Enzo difficult to deal with, she said, but he had always held his work for Driade in high esteem. He had also been the first producer to manufacture Enzo's furniture, specifically his *Sof–Sof* chair and sofa–bed *Daynight* (1971), his *Frate* table (1973), and his *Delfina* (1974). On discovering that I was a fan of Enzo Mari's work, however, Enrico sternly forbade me to use the same "sad" palette as him. He seems to have formed an impression of me as a second Enzo Mari—another minimalist like Konstantin Grcic, the German from the "Monaco di Bavaria."

I understood what he was saying. After all, like Philippe Starck and Bořek Šípek, he belonged to a different world—the world of unbridled baroque and crazy color schemes. In any case, I had yet to make it at all as a designer and in those days was still working as an exhibition maker. And just as Enrico Astori had prophesied, I would be forty before my turn came.

Enrico spent a lot of time patiently teaching me about the world of design, explaining what royalties are and how the Italian system works. He placed all his connections at my disposal, and invited me to his famous dinners where I met all sorts of people from the world of design, art, and journalism. He was exceptionally generous—at least with people with whom he saw eye to eye, which was not always predictable. He was unusually intuitive and constantly searching for novelty or for the next big thing; he always had his finger firmly on the pulse, alert to anything that was ahead of its times.

When I put it to him that Philippe Starck's *Dr. No* armchair for Kartell of 1996 perhaps bore too much of a resemblance to the *Lord Yo* armchair that he had created for Driade two years earlier, Enrico remained calm and dispassionate: "That's wonderful, because Kartell is cleverer than we are. They were able to dispense with the aluminum frame, which made their chair cheaper to make." Not a word about Starck. For him it was clear. Such things were a matter for the *imprenditore*. He was always measured, but knew very well what was going on, which is also what motivated him. That is how it was with Giulio Cappellini's *Progetto Oggetto* collection and with the aforementioned *Atlantide* and *D.House* collections. And that is also how it was at the parties on the eve of the Salone, which regularly attracted some three thousand people. The watchmaking industry had seen neck and neck challenges like that in the 1960s and 1970s, as had the automotive industry, where designers were constantly migrating from one marque to another. And now design was going the same way. What had formerly been self-evident, that a designer or architect would work only for one manufacturer, was now passé, even if I myself would remain true to this old-fashioned model for many years to come. But at least that change of mores allowed us non-Italian designers to get a foothold in the world of Italian design, whereas today the whole industry is a jungle in which coherence and integrity are thin on the ground. The era of gentlemen's agreements and gentleman entrepreneurs is over. The watchword now is opportunism.

Driade developed the *Atlantide* and *D.House* collections in response to Cappellini's *Progetto Oggetto,* which was a collection of small essential and non–essential objects of everyday use curated by James Irvine and Jasper Morrison, as far as I know. It was unveiled in 1993, when its only rival was the Danese collection. Driade's collections comprised objects both large and small for use in the home. Enrico again saw the Enzo Mari in me and commissioned me to design some small objects for *D.House* as well as two accessories for *Atlantide*.

Having by then done remunerative work for the Museum für Gestaltung Zürich, Alias, Authentics, and Thonet, I saw my fee as a matter of course. Besides, thanks to Enrico, I now knew what royalties meant and how they worked. But when I asked for several million lire (the equivalent of about 20,000 euros), he replied that he would be happy to pay that, but only as an advance on my royalties. Not only that, but I had to work fast on the two dozen objects entrusted to me. How many sleepless nights that job cost me! But it also taught me a lesson: Sure, you get your money, but you have to deliver. Henceforth, one of my first questions to a client was how soon they expected to see results. In the end, however, I managed to deliver designs for flatware and glassware, vases and dishes, wall hooks and coat-hangers, ashtrays and a CD rack.

I had arrived at the point that I had long dreamed of: that of one day working as a designer for an Italian manufacturer! The objects may have been small, but they were numerous, and they were for Driade—just five years after founding my studio. What it takes? You have to have a dream, a vision, and persistence, as well as faith and confidence in yourself, not to forget the courage to go after happiness. I chose to focus on what I knew well. The *Vis-à-Vis* ashtray, for example, referenced the abstract *Cubo* that Bruno Munari designed for Danese, while the *Rosa Simple* dish, the *C-Hook* fold-down wall hook, and *Jim* desk trays were all inspired by works by Enzo Mari. That too much knowledge can be paralyzing I discovered to my cost. How could I set that knowledge aside? How could I ignore the history of design and the pressure I was under?

At the same time, I was working with new materials that could be used for industrial-scale production: extruded plastics and pressed aluminum, for example. I also learned about the downsides of industrial production. When I saw the first industrially produced *Tulip* glasses, I mistook them for prototypes and remarked on the air bubbles in the glass and the poor quality of the foot, only to be told that this was the best quality to be had for the intended retail price. Henceforth, I would insist on being able to produce several prototypes or at the very least reserve the right to approve or reject a design before it went into production. That, too, was part of my learning curve, as it is in my nature to always look ahead. Mistakes would undoubtedly be made; what mattered was not to repeat them, and not to repeat myself either. Even more important, however, was that my ideas were now being industrially produced, because I never wanted to end up like an artist without a gallery, an architect who never builds, a chef without a restaurant. I am a designer and I want to work with industry to make my ideas available to the masses.

Another story from Enrico helped shape the stance that I have retained to this day. We were talking about Ron Arad and the thematic similarities between his designs for different manufacturers. "He showed us this design years ago," Enrico remarked. "We didn't want it. And when it went into production elsewhere, I wondered to myself how many other potential producers he had gone to with the designs that he showed us." That made me prick up my ears. I had always imagined that a design came about through dialogue with different people and manufacturers, that it was a joint effort, so to speak.

Then Enrico gave me a sheet of A4 paper as his briefing for another project. He wanted my take on the famous *Folien–Schrank 385* by Kurt Thut (1993), the father of a friend and fellow designer. We would have it made in China or India, he said, as anywhere else would be too expensive. I was horrified. It was an insult to the whole industry. Besides, I had already resolved never to copy the work of a friend or fellow designer nor to do anything that even came close. None of that mattered to Enrico, however; to him it was simply my job.

Driving back from the Driade factory in Fossadello di Caorso in my bright–blue Fiat 128, I still could not believe what I had heard. But since I had again received my fee—this time on Enrico's own initiative—I spent the next few months working on a prototype that would be an improvement on the original cupboard, which incidentally now stands in the Museum für Gestaltung Zürich. The *Folien–Schrank 385* was capacious, about 60 × 60 centimeters, and very lightweight. Forwarders always invoice you for whatever costs more, weight or bulk, and in this case it was the latter. My own design was larger, and as 60 centimeters across is no longer enough for a wardrobe, I extended it to 100, while retaining the same depth, the equivalent of one coat–hanger. I gave it a floor and a ceiling and three ripstop fabric walls that could be folded up easily. There were two ladders with rungs for shelves to rest on and to keep the fabric taut, and the doors, like the frame, were made of wood. They were suspended from the frame and being covered in the same fabric looked rather like airplane wings. My presentation of the cupboard took less than two minutes. It was light, as stipulated, and I had been able to transport it in my own small car.

On seeing it, however, Enrico declared it impossible on the grounds that ripstop fabric like that was not to be had in India. The cupboard had to be made of just one material so that it could be produced by just one manufacturer and cost no more than 400 euros. I was furious. I had invested weeks of my time in this prototype, and it had been rejected in less time than it took to assemble it! The normally diplomatic Sergio Buttiglieri hid behind his beard. Devastated by this damning verdict, I dismantled the cupboard and swore to myself that never again would I accept such a briefing. Nicola Rapetti clearly felt for me and escorted me to my car, whose blue body seemed to have become one with the sky above Piacenza. The searing heat that day was hard to bear, but the crushing blow dealt out to me by Enrico even harder.

With a heavy heart, I drove the 360 kilometers back to Zurich. Why was I taking it all so personally? Even while learning my trade, I had always given every idea of mine my all. Later I learned that other designers do likewise. So this method of giving a designer an imperious thumb's up or thumb's down was not for me.

But then it occurred to me that if my work was to cost nothing, that was something that I should address head on. I called this practice of designing things for which there was no budget the "Judo Method." My idea was that we designers should embrace its negative aspect, the minimal budget in other words, and turn it to our advantage. The flow of driving enabled me to channel my thoughts, even if it was actually quite a slow flow given that, for me, the optimum noise–to–speed ratio kicks in at 110 kilometers per hour.

The answer I eventually came up with was this: For the retail price quoted I could do no more than weld four tubes together; and it was that line of thinking that gave rise to *Tauromachia*, a leaning clothes rack consisting of four tubes held together with four screws and attached to the wall and floor by four rubber suction pads. It was a typology that suited young nomads very well, as there was no other lean–to wardrobe on the market back then. I also created a piece of storage furniture that I called *Upside Down*, which for transport purposes could be reduced to half its size. Those were my last designs for Driade, however. I am profoundly grateful to Enrico Astori for all sorts of different things. What I learned from him was to influence my whole career. I have always taken my cues from artists, architects, and fashion designers who do not repeat themselves and who try to approach each new project with new eyes, with new methods and techniques, so when Enrico opined that designers always repeat themselves, he was addressing the wrong person. Yet it was still salutary for me to hear it, because it gave me a direction, pointed out the way.

Enrico Astori's death in 2020 touched me deeply. We had first met at the furniture fair of 1986 and he died in the first year in which it had to be canceled on account of the Covid pandemic. It was then, unexpectedly finding myself with time on my hands, that I decided to write about the joy of meeting people like him.

Verbal Doodling

Giulio Cappellini, the Truffle Hound

My first encounter with Giulio Cappellini, which took place years before Konstantin Grcic and Jasper Morrison introduced me to him in person, became lodged in my mind as a kind of dream–like show or drama. The year was 1986 and I was on my first visit to the furniture fair in Milan. Cappellini's scenography hit me like a bolt from the blue. It was like something from another planet that was to shape my development and my vision. I still have the catalogue, a 17 × 40–centimeter ring binder labeled *Shiro Kuramata e Cappellini. Progetti Compiuti* (1986). For me it was like entering a dream world: all that incredibly poetic furniture, the chests of drawers, the unusual proportions, all exquisitely staged in a palazzo in the center of Milan with dry ice and laser beams pointing the way, and music from Tarkovsky's movie *Stalker* to add to the mystique. It was a Salone experience *par excellence*. The ring binder contains a wonderful text by Patrizia Scarzella, who would later write for Zanotta when I was designing products for them too, and the even more beautiful words of Shiro Kuramata himself:

Alfredo Häberli

"I have loved drawers since I was a child. Mine were always full of toys, spinning tops, and color cards: my hidden treasures. I loved reaching into them and scrabbling around in them. As an adult, it occurs to me that my drawers are perhaps my way of searching for something that is no longer there, for spinning tops and color cards… or perhaps I am myself that 'something.'"

That first visit to Milan left me lost for words. I was completely bowled over by it, though in a positive sense. I knew Japan only from books borrowed from the library and there had seen the buildings by Kenzo Tange, Fumihiko Maki, Tadao Ando. So Japan was certainly on my radar; and since this was also the time when I was discovering periodicals, I had also read about it in *The Architectural Review* No. 1074 "The New Spirit," and No. 1089 "Japan," as well as in the Japan editions of *Domus* and *Interni*. As difficult as it was to obtain information, my constant traveling, my curiosity, and my fierce determination to sell myself as a budding designer and to seize any catalogue I could lay my hands on (which was not so easy in those days) enabled me to create my own cosmos.

Cappellini was a worldly–wise aesthete with exceptionally fine feelers for all things new. He was also well-connected in the world of art and fashion and one of the most important talent scouts of the era. With his charm, his good looks, and his eloquence, he had journalists the world over going into raptures. They singled him out as their guru; and not by chance, since he pulled off one fantastic show after another. He was the quintessential Italian entrepreneur: responsible, strong-willed, and very much his own person.

For years and years, Cappellini and Driade easily outshone all the other opening-night parties, attracting thousands of guests. And that same energy became my rocket fuel, too. The show staged by Paolo Pallucco and Mireille Rivier in an abandoned slaughterhouse on the outskirts of Milan at the 1988 furniture fair blew me away. The venue had been no more than swept clean and the detritus it contained simply lined up against the peeling walls. The lighting was minimalist, but its impact extremely powerful, especially in conjunction with designs such as *Barba d'Argento, Hans and Alice,* and *Tankette*! It was pure avant-garde and remains unparalleled to this day. As a design manifesto, moreover, it probably marks the birth of the Fuori Salone of the mid-1980s. It fascinated me in part because something like that would never have occurred to me. It really was something else entirely and I was awestruck by it. The trip back to the city center turned out to be almost as crazy and exciting as there were no taxis to be had for love or money. Back then, the only way of finding out where to go and what to see was to ask people directly. Those inquiries gave rise to a kind of randomly composed, word–of–mouth guide to the fair, which would probably include the showrooms on the Piazza San Babila and Via Durini with Achille Castiglioni and Vico Magistretti's interior designs for Cassina—creations like *Veranda* and *Sindbad, Feltri* and *Hilly*—as well as the display windows for Flos, the De Padova shows, and much more besides.

All those days, hours, minutes spent at the fair are still as vivid to me as if they had happened only yesterday. And the more I reflect on them, the more I remember.

Verbal Doodling

Patrizia Moroso or buongiorno tesoro

The Biennale Interieur in Kortrijk, Belgium, always invites a guest of honor, a distinction that in the course of its fifty–year history has gone to such illustrious figures as Raymond Loewy, Gio Ponti, Verner Panton, Jean Prouvé, Dieter Rams, Jasper Morrison, and Jean Nouvel. My own turn came in 2006, although that was certainly not the first time that I had taken part in the show.

My creations had been included in its 1998 "Street of Young Designers," and two years later I had contributed an installation called *How High the Moon* as well as being one of the jurors. It was on a visit to the Moroso stand at one of the Kortrijk biennials that I first met Patrizia Moroso and Patricia Urquiola, whose first work for Moroso, the *Step* sofa, remains unforgettable (and led to the moniker that we would henceforth use for them: Pati & Pati). That first meeting was funny, laid back, upbeat, witty, chaotic, joyful, crazy, and cordial all at the same time. She was surrounded by people like Alberto Gortani (Direttore Generale), Alberto

Zontone (Export Manager), Marco Cappellin (Export Manager), and Mirko van den Winkel (Export Area Manager)—a whole *armada,* in fact. My wife Stefanie and I have long been close friends of Alberto Zontone, who would later become Patricia Urquiola's life partner and share a studio with her.

Encounters like that one with Pati & Pati were not just relevant and important—they were actually vital. Not that I was fishing for a job or a joint project, as my interest was always in the people themselves. This also explains how I arrived at my strategy of working only for people I like, so that the only awkwardness to arise is in figuring out how to combine the professional with the personal.

Patrizia and I met again at the next Salone in Milan, and again it was like meeting a kindred spirit. I am not so much younger than she is, yet whenever I talk to her on the phone, I always feel as if I'm talking to Mama. She is so generous, so empathetic, so kind–hearted—so there. "Buongiorno tesoro," she always says in that deep, sonorous voice of hers on the telephone. And eventually I did receive an inquiry from Moroso, only not what I had expected. It was put to me in 2002, the year of its fiftieth anniversary, and the task was to submit a file with a Moroso–compatible design for rapid prototyping on a scale of 1:10. It could be anything. I had *carte blanche.* The only requirement was that the file be readable. That marked the beginning not just of our collaboration, but also of the new technology of rapid prototyping. Franca Sozzani and Patrizia Moroso had invited fifty famous designers, including figures from the world of fashion like Jean Paul Gaultier, Hussein Chalayan, and Yohji Yamamoto but also architects like Michele de Lucchi and Jean Nouvel, and product designers like Tom Dixon and Javier Mariscal. For me it was a great honor to be invited to contribute to this anniversary event and the touring exhibition *Off–Scale.*

Since I was traveling a lot at the time and being a young father was zapping my energies, I often caught myself wanting to be left in peace, wanting to press "Pause." But it was also then that I read a book about the German artist and Bauhaus master Paul Klee, who said that drawing was like taking his pencil for a walk. That prompted me to draw my wing–back chair with footrest, *Take a Line for a Walk,* the outline of which I sent to Moroso as a file for rapid prototyping. When Patrizia's uncle Marino Moroso—"Zio Moroso," as I called him—saw it, he was so taken with the idea that he decided to make the prototype on a scale of 1:1. I flew to Venice two weeks later, and after a few tweaks and minor adjustments (its 80–centimeter–long wings had to clipped!) it went into production. This practice of working first on models and sketches and then refining them through dialogue remained the classic "Moroso Method." This was how Patrizia and the prototyping department developed their projects. It was like sculpting, and almost all of it on a scale of 1:1 or on the product itself. This is also how we proceeded on our last project together, *Taba* (2020).

This very different approach, this eye for forms, is a special gift that sets Patrizia Moroso apart from all the other remarkable *gran imprenditore*—or in her case *gran signora imprenditrice*—whom I encountered. As in many other lines of business, it is rare to find a woman in this role. Of course, there were and still are exceptions. Maddalena De Padova, for example, was just such a lady, endowed with good instincts and a sure sense of Scandinavian design, especially the sleek simplicity of Dieter Rams. She was also the life partner of Vico Magistretti, perhaps the most elegant architect in Milan, an old–school gentleman. While Maddalena and I were both jurors in Kortrijk and later worked on a project together, I never actually met Vico. Patricia Urquiola also collaborated with Magistretti and did some work for De Padova. That was where I first spotted her name, in fact. At last another woman! While there have indeed been some wonderful women in the history of Italian design—Franca Helg, Gae Aulenti, Cini Boeri, Anna Castelli Ferrieri, and Nanda Vigo all spring to mind—they remain relatively rare.

The Milanese are prone to a certain arrogance, believing themselves to be superior to their compatriots from the Veneto and even more from the south. What they underestimate, however, is the energy and drive of those who come from outside the establishment. Patrizia Moroso has that energy. And she also has incredibly fine feelers for people, for proportions, and for trends. Regional distinctions never mattered to me, but they were very much in evidence in Milan—what with Memphis and postmodernism, Sottsass, Mendini, Branzi and Graves, Rossi, Hollein— and *Domus,* as always, in the thick of it. While Vitra and Rolf Fehlbaum were also big on first editions, including those of Coop Himmelb(l)au, Ginbande, Arad, and Kuramata, the Italians were great at scenography, masters of the art of selling things, and of securing a spot on the map of design history—over and over again. Sometimes deservedly so, sometimes not.

Alfredo Häberli

When Christian Brändle, the new director of the Museum für Gestaltung Zürich, first spoke of his wish to stage a monographic exhibition of my work and to supplement it with two panel discussions, I gave him the names of some people whom he might want to invite. This resulted in two wonderful events: "The Long Path to the Product" with Patrizia Moroso, Patricia Urquiola, Konstantin Grcic, and myself, moderated by the design journalist Karianne Fogelberg, and "Design Development: Always One Step Ahead?" with Adrian van Hooydonk, Ross Lovegrove, Ascan Mergenthaler, and myself, moderated by Renate Menzi, curator of the design collection.

All those moments of togetherness—those first exhibitions outside Switzerland, the private viewings with fellow designers, the birthday parties, the awards ceremonies, the book launches, the births of our children, the studio openings, the car races, the juries—all those moments spent in the company of friends bound together by our shared passion for design, especially in Milan, were for me the best possible proof that yes, you can count on chance. They were also moments of true happiness.

Verbal Doodling

The Invisible Ones — il famoso ufficio tecnico

When I began working for Italian firms, I soon became aware of how important it is to get to know the employees—all those invisible people who do such excellent work, who are simply there as a matter of course. Yet they are anything but a matter of course! On the contrary, these are people who understand us designers, who support us, drive us, and make our visions come true. They are often designers themselves, while others are architects, engineers, or even mechanics. Thirty years ago, the typical *ufficio tecnico*—technical department—consisted of just one or maybe two people: one to take care of the mechanical aspects and prototyping, and one to handle the production and pricing of the end product.

The people in such positions generally have one extremely important character trait: They are modest and happy to work behind the scenes for someone else—their boss or the designer or both. It is precisely this quality that makes them so indispensable. They are often the ones who pick me up at the station or the airport or who fetch coffee and water at the start of a meeting.

And because of their own professional background and experience, they are able to follow what we are saying, to latch onto an idea and run with it. Rarely has such a person ruled any idea of mine unfeasible, and then only with good grounds that turned out to be correct. Technical department staff are not lackeys slavishly following instructions to the letter. On the contrary, their job is not an easy one and I have always had tremendous respect for them.

Many of them became friends and allies, without whose support I could not have seen an idea through to completion. And if others tried to interfere with our work, it was the technical department people who deflected or placated or appeased them so that we could get on with our task. Their knowledge of producers, manufacturing methods, and the best mold- and model-makers—to say nothing of the best restaurants in the region—is of inestimable value both to the firms they work for and to the realization of great designs.

Thinking about it, what strikes me is not only how adept at spotting ideas these people are, but also how articulate. They are great speakers— design history personified. So talking to them about the many designers they have encountered and their methods is always fun. Many of them are still at it, while others have since gone their own way, though they remain part of my history and dear friends. I am thinking here of people like Martina Karmelina, Tiziano Colico, Paolo Reina, Daniele Greppi, Stefano Barbazza, Vittorio Libertucci, Sergio Buttiglieri, Amadeo Cavalchini, Nicola Rapetti, Esra Ohl, Fiorella Gussoni, Marino Moroso, Andrea Sanguinetti, Enrico Perrin, Daniele Zamò, Giorgio Capone—to name but a few.

Verbal Doodling

Konstantin Grcic and Jasper Morrison — Sketching Our Own Landscape

My research for the exhibition *Bruno Munari—Far vedere l'Aria* at the Museum für Gestaltung Zürich that kept me busy from 1993 to 1995 brought me into contact with a number of interesting people. It was then that I got to know Jacqueline Vodoz and Bruno Danese, who had founded the Milanese firm of Danese back in 1957. Both were driven by their fascination with art and design; hence the series of exhibitions of Marco Romanelli, Marco Ferreri, Manuela Cirino, Salvatore Licitra, and others curated by Jacqueline and Bruno with a tie–in booklet by Italo Lupi, who happened to live close by.

Their 1994 exhibition was called *Oggetto Ambiente* and was held at a place on Via Maria Fulcorina, just around the corner from Hotel Speronari. I drove there in my trusty Fiat 128 and parked nearby. The reason I remember that one show so well is that it was there that I first met Konstantin Grcic, the designer from "Monaco di Bavaria," which I later learned is what the Italians call Munich. His intriguing contribution to the exhibition gave us a foretaste of his prodigious talent and intellect. Called *1 + 1 = 1,* it comprised a table that could be pushed through a wall, serving as a bookcase on one side and as a bare wall on the other. All that I had known of Grcic prior to that was what I had gleaned from Marco Romanelli's piece in *Domus* No. 754 of 1993. Seeing his works for SCP and the prototypes illustrating that article, I instantly felt a certain kinship for him, and over the years we did indeed become good friends. We were constantly crossing each other's paths, and we shared the young initiate's sense of wonder at all the new things we were discovering. Making full use of our connections, we sauntered through Milan together and trawled the trade fair booths in both Frankfurt and Cologne. Pooling what we had learned was also important to us, as back then we had no idea how business actually worked. It was again Konstantin who introduced me to Jasper Morrison. It was actually that same evening, at that same event, where Jasper was presenting a free–standing, U–shaped shower with a washbasin on one arm of the U, a place to hang clothes on the other, and a table at the rear.

Jasper was another designer I knew mainly from an article in *Domus* No. 694 of 1988 and

Alfredo Häberli

Intramuros; I had also read the book *Jasper Morrison—Design, Projects and Drawings, 1981–1989,* and at the Architectural Association bookstore in London I had purchased ten of his *A World Without Word*s booklets of 1992 with the intention of using them as gifts. My mania for magazines and books was already there.

So that was how I made the acquaintance of two designers whom I admired right from the start. Years later, when Jasper was at Vitra in Switzerland, he called to ask if I fancied going for a beer. The beer came with a request attached: Did I happen to have any of those AA booklets still in my possession? He must have recalled my talking about them and asking him why he had chosen products by Enzo Mari as illustrations. I later checked on my bookshelf and found five copies. We then agreed to meet for a beer in the old town of Zurich, and by the time I got there Jasper was already sitting at the table, waiting patiently for me to arrive. I had brought along two of the books, but gave him only one of them, which he then used as the basis for Lars Müller's reprint of 1998. I asked Jasper to repay me by writing a dedication in the second copy that I had brought along with me, and this he gladly did, since he himself no longer had any copies at all of that first edition. His dedication read: "For Alfredo, Thanks for the other one! Jasper." I spent much less time with Jasper than with Konstantin. But we shared some very special, unspectacular moments of great candor. The most emotional of these had to do with Ruth, but does not have to be related here.

When I one day realized that I could now live on my royalties, I told Jasper of my revelation only to receive the rather laconic response: "Welcome to the club." It is a very small club, unfortunately. Jasper always made sound professional choices and made a point of working with only a few, hand-picked firms, which is what I had always intended—and still do, even today. I noticed that Stefanie and our daughter, Aline, bought objects designed by Jasper simply because they found them attractive and desirable. Jasper could hardly hope for higher praise than that and I'm sure he appreciates it.

My discovery of Jasper Morrison the designer in fact took place much earlier, in the book *Gefühlscollagen, Wohnen von Sinnen* of 1986. I also recall seeing a sofa of his that worked with a stack of thin mats, and while I can no longer find it in the book, it is certainly lodged in my memory. I myself have a *Doorhandle I* by FSB (1166) and naturally a *Thinking Man's Chair* with handwritten dimensions, as well as a *Plywood Chair*. When Stefanie and I bought a house and began fixing it up many years ago, we chose Jasper's aluminum door set FSB 1144—his first commercial success of 1990—for our doors. Although only twelve pages long, the FSB door–handle program became a kind of Bible to me. On the cover was a black–and–white photo of Jasper. He looked very young in his sleeveless pullover and was sitting at a table in front of a Mac Classic, holding one of his "lightbulb" doorknobs. But the best page is the one with the design drawings and eight photos of his works in various shades of green, plywood, and black–and–white photography. The text reads as follows: "Among the friends and patrons of the young English designer Jasper Morrison are Aram Design, Cappellini, Neotu, SCP, and Vitra. Here are some examples of his work created in collaboration with these patrons." That was exactly what I wanted to do: to work for just a few, outstanding firms. Jasper had been doing it since 1981, whereas I had entered the ring only in 1991. The thought that I am holding "a part of him" every time I open a door is actually rather amusing. My own design for FSB 1224 went into production in 2012 at the same time as the opening of the Hotel 25hours in Zurich West.

The year 1998 marked the tenth anniversary of Jasper's collaboration with Cappellini, prompting Zona in Zurich to devote a whole exhibition to his work and to have a reprint of his door–handle program and a new pamphlet published by Lars Müller. Jasper, Alfonso Arosio, and Giulio Cappellini himself took the opportunity to pay me a visit, as Giulio had long wanted to get to know the "Swiss designer." After showing them round the studio that I occupied above a joinery not far from the Zona store, I took them on a surprise visit to what was then the Heidi Weber Museum—Centre Le Corbusier. The architect's only work in steel and the last building that he finished designing before suffering a fatal heart attack while swimming in the Mediterranean in 1965, the pavilion opened in 1967, although the plans actually date from 1963. Anyway, Jasper took along his sketchbook and using his Lamy 2000 fountain pen drew a few details in his typically precise, minimalist style. There is something spartan about his drawings, even if all the most important trajectories and ideas are there; and as with an engraving or an etching, there are no corrections. Giulio wanted to shoot the whole Cappellini collection right there in the pavilion and asked me to relay his request to Heidi Weber as the one who commissioned the building, whom I happened to know personally.

Alfredo Häberli

Although I had known Giulio since the early 1990s, it was those days we spent together in Zurich that led to our collaboration. Like many other manufacturers, Giulio saw in me the "Swiss inventor" and so asked me to design a folding chair and pull-out table. Why always these difficult tasks? I thought. Jasper had come late to an armchair, a stackable chair, and later still a folding chair, so why did I have to start with them? For me there are two kinds of folding chair: the very cheap ones that you hide away and bring out only in an emergency and then the movie director's chair made of wood and canvas.

Giulio, it turned out, had arrived at much the same conclusion. I therefore took the two H-frames of the classical movie director's chair and out of them developed two, almost minimalist I-frames made of cast aluminum. The prototypes of my *XX* folding chair and *Easy Long* table that can be pulled out with one hand were unveiled at the Areal Superstudio Più on Via Tortona as part of the 2001 Fuori Salone. They were exhibited alongside thirty other prototypes by designers such as Carlo Colombo, Piero Lisoni, Jean Marie Masseau, Christoph Pillet, Marcel Wanders, and my friends Jasper Morrison, Erwan, and Ronan Bouroullec. Inevitably, my modest, unassuming design was completely crowded out. The name Cappellini and the other designers had stirred up a lot of media attention, however, even if the press—though not the trade journals—focused mainly on Giulio himself, hailing him as a "design guru" and connoisseur. Only a fraction of the prototypes exhibited that day ever went into production—if that. One of them was the stool on wheels called *Move Away* and another the *Fold Away* table. Although I never really understood Giulio's philosophy, we generally made excuses for him, although some designers did break with him eventually.

His taste, his aesthetic, his style of product photography, his color schemes—they were different right from the start. He had a gift for scenography and for discovering new talent, and this enabled him to continue making his mark into the new millennium. He was constantly on the go, always with his ear to the ground and eyes wide open, always both well-informed and on the alert. He was a trend scout before the profession even existed, and the Italian practice of working on the prototype and on the product was Giulio's preferred method, too. There could be no cutting corners with him, and on inspecting the result he might well ask: Can we exaggerate that? Can we make that tube even thinner or extra thick? He was constantly looking for a distinctive aesthetic, something out of the ordinary, which is why the Cappellini collection for so long set the standard for all sorts of producers. It was sexy—that's my word for it at any rate.

My most touching experience with Giulio was on the stage of the Kornhaus in Bern. My *Kids' Stuff* tableware had won me the 2005 Swiss Design Prize in the "Market" category and I was there to receive my award. It was our son, Luc, who had motivated that particular creation. Konstantin had been invited to give the laudation, but had been too busy with his own work—specifically with a problem that had come up with a tool (probably for his *Chair One*). So he sent Giulio what he had written and Giulio read it out loud in his charming, heavily accented English. It was very beautiful! I still have it somewhere in my archive. When I stepped onto the stage, Giulio embraced me warmly before handing over the prize. And then it happened: I felt the pressure that had been mounting ever since I first opened my studio just fall away. The commendation of one of my best friends, read by a great *imprenditore*—that meant the world to me! And then that embrace. I was so moved I could barely say anything at all, other than to acknowledge my great debt to Stefanie, who has been at my side since our student days, who does so much for me in the background, and who has given us two wonderful children. After all, they were the reason why Iittala had commissioned me with *Kids' Stuff* in the first place. At least I managed to blurt out that one sentence, but then was simply too overcome with emotion to continue. Yet those few seconds of profound gratitude were all the affirmation I had been looking for. The hard work, the hopes, the refusal to give up—it had all been worthwhile.

Verbal Doodling

Back to My Friend and Fellow Designer Konstantin Grcic

Konstantin and I first crossed paths after we had each founded a studio in 1991 and were working on projects for the same firms and taking part in the same exhibitions and competitions. If Achille Castiglioni and Enzo Mari were the *grandi maestri* of the previous generation, then Konstantin Grcic and Jasper Morrison were the designers I most looked up to in my own—as they still are today.

Our early interactions were important as a way of learning from each other, given that back then, everything was new to us: contracts, fees, working with industry, trade fairs, PR, and the nuts and bolts of building up a studio of international renown. It was probably the most uncertain time of my career, but also the most exciting. We talked on the phone a lot—about our professional insecurities, but also about our shared passion for Formula 1. Konstantin was a great fan of Ferrari and Michael Schumacher, and even liked to sport a red Ferrari cap. So we picked apart the races in much the same way as we picked apart the designs we saw at the fairs.

Especially vivid to me is a memory from the turn of the millennium when we were walking past the Moroso booth in Milan and spotted Patricia Urquiola's *Step* sofa. We joked about the designer's name, since neither of us knew how to pronounce it, although it certainly rang a bell. Was that the friend of Patrizia Moroso, whom I had once been introduced to? The design definitely had something going for it, on that we were both agreed. The year 2000 then saw the launch of Patricia Urquiola's *Lowland* and *Lowseat,* and what a coup they were! And two years later came *Fjord.*

By now I was accommodating my assistants at Hotel Speronari, where I always prebooked a dozen or so rooms that I could then allocate at the last minute. Konstantin had initially stayed in a small apartment owned by the Vodoz–Danese family, but then switched to the Speronari for a while, before finally opting for a hotel close by, the Spadari al Duomo. That meant that we could meet for breakfast at Caffè Spadari and then walk over to the fair, having a chat along the way. The point was to learn from each other and from each other's observations. Konstantin has this great gift for putting his observations into words. His intellectual acuity is remarkable, as is his artistic sensitivity and grasp of architecture. His study of materials and technologies is at once passionate and painstaking, and he has the stamina and persistence of the whole German soccer squad. Konstantin is one who holds out to the very end—and then some. He is relentlessly sharp, but never humorless, as is evident from the various interviews and talks that he has given and of course the designs themselves. As a friend, I have come to see other sides of his character, too.

Konstantin has always been ahead of his times. Take his *Bishop* table trestles for SCP, for example, the inspiration for which I discovered only years later in a book by Shiro Kuramata containing a photo of his *Portrait Inside Out* table (1987). Then there is his *Start* chair for Cappellini (1993), which is clearly a riff on Jean Prouvé's *Chaise à assise* rabattable. Konstantin's bridges, his sources of inspiration, and his vision have always been exceptional. I have enormous respect for him, and admire him no end.

Take all the projects he did for Plank and Magis, or Eugenio Perazza—that wonderful, crazy, challenging, and passionate manufacturer from Treviso near Venice, who is such a perfect match for Konstantin's way of working. The examples of his tireless quest for the projects, typologies, and technologies of tomorrow are endless and include *Chair One, Traffic, Brut, 360°*—to name but a few. The best thing about this relationship is that Perazza had faith in Konstantin and challenged his way of working. Theirs is a unique chemistry. Konstantin shuttles back and forth between the uniqueness of an Achille Castiglioni, the engineering approach of a Richard Sapper, and the unflagging radicalism of an Enzo Mari, though not so much in the here and now as in the future.

When I first became a father twenty-three years ago, Konstantin was en route to Italy and immediately came to visit me. He wanted to support Stefanie, who had just become a mother, and who had also known Konstantin right from the start. I remember how we went for a long walk together in the woods, and how Konstantin insisted on pushing the buggy, which with the path covered in snow was no easy matter. But the delight he took in children was clearly visible. It was one of only a few encounters when we did not talk much, and even less about our work as designers. Konstantin once told me how much he admired the way I managed to juggle my design work with my relationship with Stefanie and our young family. That was balm to my soul, as building a studio of international renown was proving very challenging. These days it would probably be even harder. It is surely not by chance that so many of my fellow designers came late to fatherhood.

Konstantin and I also shared a similar approach to exhibition catalogues and the staging of our products, which for us was always an opportunity to try out new technologies, materials, and concepts; hence our constant probing, searching, grappling, and playing around in an effort to gain insights great and small, momentous and trivial. There was always something that we could turn to our advantage, and books and exhibitions remained a key source of inspiration, and still do today.

We also took part in the same exhibitions, sometimes as representatives of our respective countries, as at the 1999 *Essential Deluxe* Exhibition in Lisbon, and sometimes actually collaborating, as we did for Moroso at *Malmö ist in Langenthal* held as part of the Designers' Saturday series in the Swiss town of that name in 2004, and with *Bubenzimmer* for the *Neue Räume* show in Zurich in 2005. Another bond between us was the interview with me— we called it a "dialogue"—that I included in my first book, *Sketching My Own Landscape*

(2002). Konstantin was also among the designer friends from Sweden, Finland, Germany, Italy, and Spain who attended my fortieth birthday party at the Restaurant Italia in Zurich, which ended with the police kindly reminding us of the time.

Financially, Konstantin himself was at last able to breathe easily only after his studio was awarded a major contract for Krups. On one occasion, when we were once again lurching from exhibit to exhibit—probably during the show *This Side Up* at the Museum für Gestaltung—I remember how we happened to pass a bookstore that he just had to enter, as I myself generally do with bookstores. This time, however, I was ordered to wait outside, while Konstantin bought me four books by Luigi Colani. That was his surprise and his way of thanking me for the many invitations that I had extended to him in Milan during the first fifteen years of my studio. I was fortunate in having been able to live on my royalties even early on in my career. The financial aspect of our profession is one that is not talked about enough. Even Jasper had not been able to invest properly in computers until after the tram project for Hanover. But that is the price that those who refuse to be mainstream have to pay.

Alfredo Häberli

I have now had my studio for thirty years, and between 1986 and 2019 I have visited the Salone del Mobile in Milan thirty-three times and have seen Konstantin there almost every time. Between fairs, however, we tend to be too busy with our own projects and appointments to meet up—at least now that we are both at the zenith of our popularity as designers. When the Speronari closed, moreover, our hotels were no longer just a few meters apart.

For me the most perilous period of all was when it seemed that I had made it into the pantheon, that I was now one of the stars. The demand for me in person, for my presence in the media, the many projects on offer, the parties—it all took its toll on my soul.

With the guardrails no longer there, I was losing control, allowing my focus to become blurred. It was then that my intoxication with the designer's life and the wonders of the Salone peaked, then that it all became too much, too big, the events too manic—and me in the midst of it. The *sprezzatura* had gone. *Sprezzatura* is sometimes described as a form of defensive irony, as "a mask of apparent restraint and nonchalance hiding what you really want, feel, think, or intend."

So I had to scale back, to become more disciplined, to concentrate on just a few events, to avoid the hype, and to relinquish quantity for the sake of true quality. Jasper was already a master of this; Konstantin suffered rather more, and I was utterly helpless—at least for a while.

What had begun as breakfast with Konstantin over coffee and a *cornetto* at the Caffè Spadari Le Tre Marie on Via Torino, the extension of Via Speronari, continued at the wonderful dinners hosted by Kvadrat, Alias, Vitra, Moroso, *T* magazine, or Hermès. Some of those banquets were held in palazzos outside the city center, others on showroom patios, in exclusive restaurants, or in private homes. They were strictly for friends only—for small, almost clandestine groups. They filled me with happiness and gratitude: I was back on track.

Verbal Doodling

Anders Byriel or Hygge in Milan

I can no longer remember exactly where I first met Anders Byriel. It was probably at a booth at some fair in Milan or Stockholm around the turn of the millennium. Anders had been at the family–run Kvadrat since 1992, initially as Head of Global Sales and from 1998 onwards as CEO. I for my part already had a foot in the door of Italian manufacturers such as Alias *(SEC, 1997)*, Cappellini *(Move Away, 2000)*, Edra *(Wing, 1999)*, Driade *(Tauromacchia, 1997)*, and Zanotta *(Ricreo, 1998)*, and had also done some designs for Scandinavian firms like Iittala *(Origo, 1999)*, Offecct *(Solitaire, 2000)*, and Asplund *(Knot, 2001)*.

Anyway, Anders and I got talking and I told him of my dream of one day doing some work for Kvadrat, although I would have to wait eight years for that dream to come true. By then, of course, we had gotten to know each other well. Anders asked me what I was doing that evening and I told him that apart from a nightcap at the Bar Basso I had no official engagements; I wanted to be free to see as many exhibitions and showrooms as possible. He then asked if I spoke French and whether

I would have time to attend the Kvadrat dinner. I answered both questions in the affirmative and later on made my way to the Osteria Del Binari on Via Tortona. Although still the new kid on the block, I was seated between Andrée Putman, the *grande dame* of interior design, and Jean Nouvel. My French dried up instantly, especially when Andrée Putman made her entrance—impeccably coiffed and clad in a long gown. What stature, what charisma! I had gotten to know Meret Oppenheim in the 1980s and had met Zaha Hadid first in London, then at the ETH in Zurich, and later still at one of the designers' dinners hosted by Vitra. All three women were incredibly charismatic and had a powerful aura of personal strength and dignity.

French was not Kvadrat's strong suit in those days, so Anders was grateful for my presence, and I, in turn, was grateful to Anders for those annual invitations to the Kvadrat dinners. This friendship had been rumbling on for eight years when I finally received the inquiry I had been hoping for: Would I design Kvadrat's new showroom in Milan and three new fabric collections along with it? What a dream job!

I knew the location on Corso Monforte well, and much to Anders's amazement was able to

Alfredo Häberli

describe it to him over the phone. But how could he have known of my close ties to Sandra Latis and Italo Lupi at *Abitare,* whose offices in those days were on the opposite side of the courtyard, where the Flos showroom designed by Jasper Morrison now stands? The only snag was the limited time available: The telephone call came in November 2006 and my designs had to be ready for the Salone of April 2007. I decided to begin by gutting the space, transforming it from a nightmare into a walk–in dream on two levels: a gallery with five workspaces and a ground floor space with room for all the fabrics and drapes as well as tables for meetings, a storeroom, and a lounge. The idea was to make Kvadrat's connection to fabrics clearly visible from the courtyard. The showroom was to be the scene of several remarkable shows during the furniture fair, and the parties held there attracted a lot of attention. Thirteen years later I redesigned it, but this time exclusively as a showroom.

Meanwhile there were all those fantastic Kvadrat dinners. Anders is a generous person: gentle, calm, empathetic, intelligent, well–read. The way he and Mette Bendix run Kvadrat as a family firm is truly exemplary. He keeps the hierarchy flat, makes full use of his employees' individual strengths and areas of expertise, and keeps them motivated. And all of this in the best Scandinavian fashion—relaxed, precise, not loud.

When I was chosen to be guest of honor at Kortrijk and given 5,000 square meters of space in which to stage an exhibition of my own, I seized the opportunity to incorporate a few other things too. I selected 280 objects from the fantastic design collection of the Museum für Gestaltung Zürich and also made a book in which I asked Swiss artists to stage my own design products for me. The artists I approached—Shirana Shahbazi, David Renggli, Walter Pfeiffer, Roman Signer, John M Armleder, Körner Union, and Stefan Burger—were already quite well known in Switzerland, so I needed help with the financing. Knowing that Anders had ties to the art world and is himself a great art lover, I asked him as a friend—this was before he became a client—whether Kvadrat might be willing to support my project. He thought the book an excellent idea and spontaneously agreed—on the telephone—to cover half of the six-figure sum that it was going to cost. He also suggested that I contact other sponsors for the other half, but assured me that if that did not work out, I should go back to him. Vintage Anders!

When the book was ready and our collaboration began, Anders asked me how well I knew Roman Signer, because he was interested in getting to know him personally. As it happens, Roman and his wife Aleksandra appreciate my work and we have an easygoing relationship with them. So I called Roman and asked if we could meet, and he very kindly invited us to visit him at his studio the very next day. I immediately called Anders to tell him the good news and a few hours later drove my Saab to Zurich Airport to pick him up. We then drove to St. Gallen, which is about an hour's drive away. It was a wonderful encounter between two people of comparable sophistication. Noticing that Anders knew his whole oeuvre and had watched many of his videos, Roman spontaneously gave him some books about his work as a gift. Anders for his part asked whether Roman could imagine doing something with cloth, because he wanted to donate a work by Roman Signer to the Louisiana Museum in Denmark. Roman was very moved by this. Of course, he would do it—just no advertising. The following summer, Roman and Anders met on the beach at Ebeltoft near Kvadrat's headquarters. There, Roman created his work *Tuch und Bogen* (2009), which entailed shooting a 50–meter–long bale of cloth into the sky above the beach and filming its descent. His sculpture *Haus* and action painting *Flying and Painting* followed in 2016.

Thus began a friendship that was sparked by a single question and a request for help with the language barrier at a dinner party in Milan. I am so profoundly grateful to have met all these wonderful people.

Verbal Doodling

Philippe Starck, l'homme qui ne dort pas la nuit

Strolling through Paris from Au Père Tranquille at Les Halles towards the Centre Pompidou, a graphic logo on the awning of a street–side café happened to catch my eye. As the weather was fine and the outside tables all occupied, I decided to go inside. The interior sent my heart into overdrive. At the far end was a huge, wedge–shaped staircase, wide enough to be divided by a partition at the top. The three-legged chairs had a one–piece wooden shell and leather seat cushions and were simple without being minimalist. The wood, moreover, was mahogany, like on a boat. The café was full and very, very lively. I found a free table upstairs and was utterly blown away. I ordered a lemonade and began sketching, letting my pencil and paper guide me. There were thousands of new ideas here, things I had never seen before: the huge clock, the mirrors on the wall, the lettering, the logo, the chairs, the tables with a cone as foot—and then the colors! The staircase was a greenish hue, but everything else pink or brick red, while the furnishings were dark brown and black.

After drawing for a while, I went to the restroom, which was even crazier: a lot of green glass and a faucet in the form of a pipe that came straight down from the ceiling and was held in place by wire brackets. Never before have I lingered so long in a restroom. I did feel slightly embarrassed about sketching while others were doing their business, but so what?

Back at my table I asked the waiter whether he knew who had done the interior design. He told me to ask his boss, who was manning the till downstairs. And that is how I met Monsieur Costes, who told me that the café had opened just a few days earlier and had been designed by a Frenchman from Paris called Philippe Starck. I made a note of the name and headed straight for the nearest telephone directory. And there it was in black and white: Philippe Starck, along with a telephone number and address. I no longer remember which arrondissement it was, but I knocked on his door the very next day. An elderly, unkempt man opened the door. Sure, his name was Starck, he said, but he was not *that* Starck. On returning to Café Costes near the Centre Georges Pompidou and the Stravinsky Fountain by Niki de Saint Phalle and Jean Tinguely I told Monsieur Costes of my disappointment at not finding Monsieur Starck, and he told me that the designer lived on the outskirts of Paris, in the village of Montfort–l'Amaury. Armed with the correct address, I set off by train, arriving at around midday. Montfort–l'Amaury, I then discovered to my dismay, was at the opposite end of a 3–kilometer–long, tree–lined boulevard. Summoning all the courage and French that I could muster, I asked the stationmaster for help. He confirmed that Monsieur Starck had had a lot of visitors just recently, most of them journalists and intellectuals. A friend of his then offered to take me to the Starcks' house, parked in front of which was a small black Mercedes 190 with a round sticker saying STARCK on the windshield.

Finally, I was in the right place.

It was a small, modest house, and contrary to many of the reports I later read, most definitely not a "villa." I pressed the doorbell, and although I heard it ring, no one came. Being loath to give up and dreading the long walk back to the station, I rang again and finally a woman tore open the door and immediately scolded me for having woken her. How would I like it, she asked crossly, if every design student came to my private home asking for an internship? Duly chastened, though glad to have found the right address, I set off back to the station and waited patiently for the next train back to Paris.

I would not meet Philippe Starck in person until later. It was at the Driade stand in Milan and must have been in the mid–1980s, when the Café Costes furnishings were going into production. Quite by chance—and it really was serendipity—I was helping Enrico Astori by doing some interpreting from French into Italian. Starck had attracted quite a crowd, as had Enrico Astori as his producer, and sandwiched between these two giants was some student from Switzerland… Afterwards I asked Starck if I might have his calling card, and he readily obliged. I also asked him if I could work for him, to which he replied not for him but with him. I liked that answer! He told me to fax him my best design to date, which naturally I did, although he never responded. Then one day, when I was trying for the umpteenth time to call him from a phone at the university, he really did pick up. I recognized his voice immediately. It is on the high side, almost squeaky, and with a heavy French accent, since I had addressed him in English. "Non, non, Monsieur Starck n'est pas là," he said between peals of laughter, "Monsieur Starck n'est pas là."

Unwilling to let this joke at my expense go unanswered, I made a copy of the portrait of Starck in the Baleri catalogue, Baleri having been one of the first to mass–produce his designs for President Mitterand's private apartment back in 1984. I then pasted onto it some sentences typed on my *Lettera 22,* designed by Marcello Nizzoli in 1950—

> "Ceci n'est pas une pipe.
> Ce n'est pas Philippe.
> C'est le menteur Starck.
> …"

—and faxed the whole A4–sized collage to the fax number on his card, putting an end to my hopes of ever doing an internship with him.

Starck's works were everywhere in those days. He seemed to have new chairs, sofas, and lamps at every Salone, and there was always at least something surprising or interesting among them, as there still is today. The commission from French Culture Minister Jack Lang had undoubtedly been a game–changer for Starck. Lang had invited him to design furnishings for part of the Elysée Palace, and the resulting works, "le fauteuil" *Madame* (later *Richard III*) or *Dr. Sonderbar, Vogelsang, Miss Dorn, Pat Conley,* and the table *Tippy Jackson* are among the most influential designs of the 1980s, and great favorites of mine.

I met Starck again at the Astoris' dinner parties on Via dei Chiostri, where he seemed quiet and withdrawn. And Konstantin Grcic and I met him at the tenth–anniversary dinner of the magazine *Intramuros,* founded by the wonderful woman who had invited us: Chantal Hamaide. There he was once again in the role he played best: the amiable clown and consummate entertainer so beloved of the press. His visions, however, remain unmatched.

Starck liked to say that he could design an entire hotel in a single day and a chair in just ten minutes. When I founded my studio in 1991 I thought that one design a week—fifty–two a year—should be enough to get by, but I soon had to revise that figure downwards to just one a month, or twelve a year, as something always came up in between. But I believe Starck. He is probably exceptionally gifted, and definitely slightly manic, verging on the autistic; and he is a damned good draftsman. It is certainly not my intention to be rude about him.

I spent the year 1988/89 doing an internship first with Hans (Nick) Roericht in Ulm, where I lived and worked in that very same building on the Kuhberg that Max Bill had designed for the famous design school that became such a pioneer of postwar industrial design in Germany, and then at Siemens in New York, where the emphasis was on telecommunications and medical apparatus. It was there, far removed from Paris, that I encountered Starck's first hotel, the recently opened Royalton Hotel. My experience on entering it was similar to my first glimpse of Café Costes, except that by now I was familiar with his work. Yet still the design surprised me—so much so that I took one of the silver–plated globe vases with me as a souvenir.

I'm sure Philippe will forgive me.

Ross Lovegrove — Supernatural

Verbal Doodling

Nicola Rapetti, who together with Sergio Buttiglieri and Fiorella Gussoni for many years ran the *ufficio tecnico* at Driade, soon became a good friend. Not only did he know how to turn our ideas into objects, but he also traveled extensively in Asia—both with and without Astori—in search of potential manufacturers and suppliers. Nicola was self-taught and had exceptionally fine feelers for people and for interpersonal relations. He had the kind of knowledge and sensitivities that many of us can obtain only by traveling abroad, the kind of knowledge my parents often spoke of.

In the mid-1990s Nicola took me to all the cool clubs (Plastic, Elephant), all the interesting bars (ATM, Atomic), and all the really good restaurants (YAR, and the Bistrot Russo, run by the son of Massimo Morozzi) in Milan, and if he was also my bodyguard, then certainly not just mentally, since in the course of his travels he had also learned how to kickbox. But I once had to defend *his* honor, too—at one of the Astoris' dinner parties. After many years on the job, he eventually left Driade, perhaps to work for Starck (who held his knowledge and knowhow in high esteem) or for Cassina or Dedon in Barcelona; or perhaps he started his own business—I can no longer remember. But at the dinner party at which I came to his defense, I was sitting next to Astori when he remarked: "Nicola will always be a boxer." Perhaps he resented his leaving, but it was still a hurtful, disparaging thing to say, especially coming from such a cultured gentleman. I refuted his assertion vehemently by saying that I had tremendous respect for Nicola as a man of great knowledge and skill and would not tolerate my friend being talked about so dismissively. And with that I stood up and left.

Nicola and I often hit the town together and sometimes stayed out all night. I doubt if many of the designers visiting from abroad did that, but one who did was Ross Lovegrove. The Sean Connery of the design scene—charming, charismatic, good-looking—Ross is an incredibly good orator, who actually likes public-speaking and is amazingly good at articulating his visions. He speaks English with a Welsh accent and is also conversant in Italian and French, even if his vocabulary is limited.

He once invited Nicola and me to the Four Seasons Hotel on Via Gesù. The lobby was already half full with a group from Texas (makers of titanium sheet) as well as customers, friends, journalists, and assistants from all over the world. Ross was in his element: talkative, welcoming, expansive, and he seemed to know all the hotel's waiters and concierges by name. He had taken off his shoes and obviously felt very much at home. Then we were joined by Gaetano Pesce from New York, whose *Feltri* project for Cassina (1987) had been an important inspiration for my graduation project in felt. Pesce was invariably experimental, invariably thought outside the box, and was constantly trying out new technologies, as he had done when he made his debut with the wonderful inflatable chair *Up* (1969). Ross, too, is a crazy designer who is similarly impossible to pin down.

Since we worked for the same firms, for Driade, Luceplan, Moroso, and Zanotta, I often had the pleasure of meeting him. I also used to attend the Geneva Motor Show press days and remember running into him there with a whole entourage of Japanese, many of them armed with cameras and avidly filming Ross as he held forth, explained, posed. It was crazy. Then he spotted me and introduced me. The Japanese, it turned out, were from the magazine *Brutus,* which was doing a piece on him. I went on my way, leaving Ross to his show, though we agreed to meet up later.

As car designers, it seems, do not all congregate in the same bar the way we did at the Bar Basso, I had to ask a Genevan journalist friend of mine where to meet. She suggested the Demi Lune, so it was there that Ross and I hung out together, lingering until very late, enjoying the drinks and each other's company as the only furniture designers around. I had invited along some car designers, too, including Adrian van Hooydonk and Chris Bangle, but unlike us they all had to get back to their hotels. It was because Ross and I had no further obligations that I managed to miss the last train back to Zurich. Realizing it was going to be a long night, we asked the lady behind the bar where else we could go for more drinks. She took one look at Ross—white hair, dark tan, long leather coat, colorful silk shirt, some kind of snakeskin pants—and gave us an address nearby, which turned out to be a gay nightclub! Ross was shocked, although the hours we spent there in the company of two Spanish women, who also seemed to have washed up there by accident, were in fact very enjoyable.

In the end, Ross invited me to camp out in his hotel suite. When his wife Miska called next morning, Ross gave me the receiver. "Ciao! Alfredo here," I said. Dead silence at the other end! It must have lasted seconds but felt like minutes. What was she thinking? Worse still, I'd known Miska for years! And we were probably still tipsy from the night before. At least I had managed to get in a few hours of sleep and was now ready to head back to Zurich. On descending the staircase into the lobby, however, we discovered that the *Brutus* crew and party of Japanese were already there waiting for us. One glance at the two of us was enough to make them lower their eyes and start giggling. That was probably my most amusing encounter with Ross. He really is a crazy, but also an excellent designer. And always impeccably dressed—a walking advertisement for design. I myself, of course, was wearing the same clothes as the night before.

Ross and I were always able to talk openly with one another. He had much more experience of industry than I did, and I frequently asked him for advice on matters relating to fees. This was a subject that had barely been touched on during our training, yet to us designers as service providers is of fundamental importance. Besides, the standard practice differed greatly from Italy to Germany, and from Finland to Japan. In those days there were no books on the subject and no Google, although Ross had a very clear idea of how much designers are worth and what our work should cost. He designed perfume flacons for the fashion industry, watches, and bottles (the finest mineral water bottle there is), and he was involved in some of the same joint projects for Italian manufacturers as I was. He understood the world of industrial design, though not that of furniture design, which was my area of expertise. It made no sense to him that fashion designers should command a fee of millions and have a huge team at their disposal whereas we had to finance all our development work ourselves, and that if there was a fee at all, it was bound to be relatively small. That made him livid.

Ross really is the most passionate designer I know, and he stakes absolutely everything on seeing his visions, his dreams, his inventions through to completion. He is "positively wild," as he himself puts it. His Studio X, which he founded in 1990, is crammed full of objects, studies, prototypes, research materials, and models. The only other studios that come anywhere close, at least to my knowledge, are those of Ólafur Elíasson in Berlin and of Luigi Colani, whom I met on two occasions: once at a talk that a friend was giving at Phonak (now Sonova Holding) and once with Albrecht Bangert at the launch of his book *Colani—Die Kunst, Zukunft zu gestalten* (Colani: The Art of Shaping the Future) in Milan. I did once speak to him on the phone while still a student, however.

Colani was most definitely an agent of design. "I have ideas for at least five hundred years," he liked to say. Colani was certainly a pioneer, just as Ross Lovegrove is, too.

Verbal Doodling

The Journalists — Word Acrobats and Linguistic Architects

They are verbal acrobats, architects who build with words, who draw with sentences, who spot things in our designs or discover facets of them that we did not consciously put there; they are people who practice a profession that has room for poetry. In Italy, especially, many journalists are literally architects who have moved sideways.

Those who wrote for the trade journals in the 1990s typically took their time, doing extensive research in an effort to find out as much as possible. Answering their questions was often quite a challenge for a young designer. The publications themselves were serious, and in their choice of photographs, sketches, and technical data were very much on a par with each other. Perhaps that is why I still have so many periodicals from that time stashed away in my studio.

Today it is different, sadly. Journalists now send us questions and hope for answers right away. The questions arrive on Thursday, say, and the answers are needed by Friday morning. You could say that we have become estranged, just as I have become estranged from the sales people in furniture stores. Why do they know so little about us designers, about the history of design, and about the period in which their wares were created?

But I still admire journalists for their linguistic skills, both in my own field and in their coverage of current affairs. If an article is well written, I immediately look to see who wrote it. Perhaps one reason for my admiration is that despite having five languages and one dialect, I cannot speak any of them perfectly. I also wonder whether a thought, to be perfect, first has to be perfectly articulated in the brain, which is a question that has haunted me ever since the Schule für Gestaltung rejected me on account of my poor German.

An article in a trade journal used to be worth its weight in gold, especially in my younger years when I was still unknown. And getting something published in a trade journal mattered a lot to critics, too. Designers are people who are written about, of course; we do not write articles ourselves. The effect of an article about you in a trade journal was equivalent to that of garnering thousands of likes and followers on social media. Making it onto the title page, moreover, was a tremendous ego boost, and conversely a source of anxiety when it did not happen. Architects and designers began hiring PR professionals in the 1980s, but I still have to smile whenever someone in my studio calls for a PR department.

What bothered me most were those architects who worked first as journalists, then as curators, and then did a bit of design themselves. For me, such a blurring of professional boundaries and the inevitable conflict of interests would be worse than no publicity at all. My own professional integrity simply would not allow it. It would be like a design prize where the sponsors' submissions are the first to be considered. That's just not done. But the Italian media, manufacturers, and design industry were never quite so fastidious, as Enrico Astori explained to me. I still find that impossible to accept.

But I have remained a book and magazine maniac to this day, and I still go out hunting for them at every opportunity—watches, too, and art, if rather less so. That makes me all the more delighted to see journalists curating even specialist books and niche exhibitions. Changes in the media mean that there are fewer and fewer of them, even though solid reporting is actually vital to public discourse. The 1980s saw high–level discussions between architects and artists, which owing to the encroachments of advertising have been steadily watered down.

Perhaps the most expensive book I bought as a young designer was *Design ist unsichtbar,* which was published as a tie–in with an exhibition at the Forum Design in Linz in 1981; today it might be the book by Peter Zumthor that was published by Lars Müller and then instantly pulped; or the old Jean Prouvé books; or the Museum für Gestaltung catalogues on the Citröen DS, *Industrieware* by Wilhelm Wagenfeld, Josef Hoffmann, Richard J. Neutra, Hans Bellmann, *Die verborgene Vernunft, Architecture en France.* It is not what they cost in second–hand bookstores that makes me cherish them; it is rather what these books meant to me at the time I first read them or first set eyes on them.

The books about Zanotta, *Mobili come Architetture,* about Danese, *Arte industriale,* about Kartell, *Plastiche e Design,* and about Alessi, *Il bel metallo,* were all formative works for me, and also the reason why I asked Stefano Casciani to write something about my work in the book *Alfredo Häberli Design Live.*

How I would love to do a book with Beppe Finessi, who for some time now has been editor-in-chief of the wonderful magazine *Inventario,* and who also wrote the "Museo Possibile" column for *Abitare.* He ranks among the true thinkers and connoisseurs of the design world and is also, quite literally, a poet. His texts make him the Lucio Dalla or Pablo Neruda of design journalism, and reading them is always a pleasure. Subtle and courageous critiques, such as those penned by Cristina Morozzi and Francesca Picchi, are also a gift. These days I find such top-notch critiques mainly in the *New York Times' T* magazine, in the *Financial Times'* magazine *How to Spend It,* or in the weekly magazines of both *Die Zeit* and *Süddeutsche Zeitung.* But thoughtful pieces on design and constructive criticism have become a rarity, and that makes the old editions that I keep in my studio all the more valuable—including as an extension of my own thoughts and memories.

Atelier, Studio, Office as Wunderkammer

Verbal Doodling

Imagine several pinboards with objects from all over the world—new, old, discontinued, found, gifted, purchased, made of all sorts of different materials, in all shapes, sizes, and colors, not categorized or in any particular order, just carefully pinned up—and add to that the endless shelves bearing still more objects, magazines, and books, the black boxes full of manufacturers' prospectuses, valuable old catalogues, materials, samples, and archive boxes; not to forget the shelves laden with historical chairs along with my own prototypes and cardboard models, some scaled down, others 1:1; a bicycle, and an almost sixty-year-old wooden boat made here on Lake Zurich; and in their midst a 100 × 300–centimeter table for my assistants, a workshop, a cutting table, my own private office partitioned off behind glass, a Donald Judd *Chair No. 1* in copper, a sculpture by Sophie Taeuber–Arp, an Imi Knoebel and Remy Zaugg on the wall, an original drawing by Flavio Manzoni, a Le Corbusier lithograph, photos by Walter Pfeiffer, models from the Kvadrat showroom in Milan, models

Alfredo Häberli

of the installation I did as guest of honor at Kortrijk, model automobiles, sculptures, photos of my own personal idols: Achille Castiglioni, Enzo Mari, Ettore Sottsass, Stefanie, Villa Malaparte, Sarah Morris. It is a light–flooded space whose large terrace looks out onto Lake Zurich. It is an orderly chaos. It is inspiration. It is a true *Wunderkammer*.

For me as a designer, my studio is not just a space. It is at once an atelier, refuge, chamber of secrets, and wellspring of inspiration. This is where I realize my ideas—ideas that one day will be shown to the world in the form of drawings, scale models, and prototypes, as well as ideas that are just as important but end up in the trash can, both literally and metaphorically.

The studio is a personal space in which I am free to experiment, to make mistakes, to be vulnerable. The studio should be a place where you never have to defend your creations. After all, there are just as many ways of being a designer as there are designs, which is why there is no archetypal design studio. Some call it a studio, others an atelier, workshop, agency, or office. Viewed in this light, it could be anywhere a designer lives, works, and dreams.

I need this setting, this space, this place as somewhere to return to from my visits to factories, from talks, trade fairs, and travels. Even as a student, it was important to me to have my table, my objects, my magazines, my books, pens, and pencils: a workshop in miniature, a setting in which I feel comfortable. And for the ideas to flow, I have to feel good, have to feel good about myself. Having the right assistants is equally important. After all, we're a team and there should be no unresolved issues between us. The fewer of us there are the better. Relations with clients are also a key factor in creating the kind of climate that is conducive to success.

The early years of my studio were tough, despite the work still coming to me from the Museum für Gestaltung. That its director Martin Heller became my friend and mentor so early on in my career was indeed an incredible stroke of luck and a huge help. But when I realized one day that I had completely miscalculated and that I could not pay my rent, my taxes, and all my other expenses, and saw my hopes of a life as an independent designer trickling away, I had no choice but to swallow my pride, and in all humility to ask my in-laws for a loan (the thought of asking my own parents being even more unbearable). My in-laws very kindly lent me a five-figure sum. My father-in-law insisted on a formal contract and gave me two years for repayment instead of the three months that I had asked for. I hated having to do that, and the moment I repaid the loan half a year later swore that never again would I allow myself to become indebted. That it was Stefanie who was already having to guarantee our survival in those early years was bad enough; hence my assertion that you need five to ten years to make a name for yourself and get established as a designer.

I was fortunate in having a chance to peek inside the studios of some of Milan's great designers, and frequently visited Bruno Munari and Enzo Mari at work. Munari gladly showed me his studio when I was preparing the exhibition about him for the Museum für Gestaltung, and it was on my second visit to Mari's studio that I realized that my idea of a joint exhibition of him and Munari based on the Jacqueline Vodoz and Bruno Danese collection would not work, and that to do them justice I would have to do a separate show for each of them in turn. That is how *Bruno Munari: Making Air Visible* began. As Mari already had an exhibition in Barcelona in 1999, *Enzo Mari, el treball al centre,* it did not make sense for me to do another one in parallel. Far and away the best and most comprehensive exhibition about Mari, however, was the one at the Milan Triennale 2020. Tragically, Enzo died the day after its opening, only to be followed by his life partner, Lea Vergine, the very next day. I was in mourning for several days—until a memory sprang to mind that seemed to bring our friendship back to life.

I went to Milan twice to see the exhibition. The first time, it was a Sunday. I drove my 1977 Porsche over the Gotthard and parked right in front of the Triennale. Because of the Covid–19 pandemic, there was already a long line in front of the ticket desk. So looking as purposeful as possible, I simply marched to the head of the queue and claimed to be just picking up an order from the bookstore. I did in fact buy several books, and realized then that I could go straight from the bookstore to the ticket desk, meaning that my strategy had paid off. I bought a ticket and entered the exhibition, and by the time I came out again it was already dusk and my platinum–colored 911 was gleaming in the twilight right in front of a poster for

Alfredo Häberli

the show. Enzo would have scolded me for coming by car, I thought. And as if losing him were not bad enough, there was also the breaking news of the Italian president's announcement that Italy was going back into lockdown.

The press conference with two dozen journalists scheduled for the next day at which I was to present my revamping of the Kvadrat showroom on Corso Monforte—my second remodeling of that space in thirteen years—was immediately canceled.

The news was brutal, but real, as Enzo's death the day after the opening had proved. I drove straight back to Zurich and to the Kronenhalle, where I dined on Züri–Geschnetzeltes mit Röschti while leafing through the two catalogues: one with Enzo's *Hammer & Sickle,* the other with the *Red Apple.*

My second visit took place during the greatly scaled back furniture fair that had been postponed until September 2021. I knew many of the early works of art only from reproductions, so it did me good to see them again. But when I saw all the notes, sketches, and other objets trouvés from the Studio Enzo Mari e Associati snc, I could not help but see the man himself sitting at his desk, the Piazzale Baracca at his back and on the right the blackboard where he had drawn all those diagrams during that unforgettable first lecture. The sight so tugged at my heartstrings that I teared up. Fortunately, I was completely alone in the room, the curator and director Marco Sammicheli having very kindly switched on the lighting an hour before the official opening so that I could view the exhibition in peace. What an honor that was. And what a leave–taking.

Enzo Mari still owed me a drawing, but he had refused to draw just anything. All that I am left with, therefore, are his letters with the letterhead "Enzo Mari e Associati snc" and a hand–drawn arrow pointing left, the books that he copied for me, and the *Anfora* vase that he gave me when he spotted me among the spectators at the stand of the Königliche Porzellan–Manufaktur Berlin in Frankfurt. "A cylinder made of porcelain and the discovery at a stroke of a form that is always different, but deeply expressive every time. Making things by hand means first and foremost thinking by hand," he had said back then.

Visiting exhibitions and the studios of fellow designers, artists, and architects is just as much a source of inspiration as visiting factories and production facilities. But perhaps my most memorable visit to a studio was the one I made just a few days after graduating, when I went to Achille Castiglioni's legendary studio on Piazza Castello in Milan.

I had graduated with flying colors, the best of my year, and consequently was in seventh heaven. I had been able to show that I could do good work, even without good German. I felt vindicated and felt this deep need to thank Achille Castiglioni in person, it having been his work, his exhibition, his personality that had inspired me to embark on the study of design.

So I called his studio and was put through to the man himself. After explaining that I had just graduated and that his work had been central to both my choice of subject and my success in it, I asked if I might have coffee with him. Would ten minutes be sufficient, he wanted to know. Of course, I said. Achille then invited me to visit him at his studio the following afternoon.

I remember it all so clearly: the doorbell, the window bars, the large mirror, the archive boxes labeled with stenciled lettering, the adjustable drawing board. The secretary brought us coffee and Achille began removing some objects from a glass case and expounding on them. The book I already knew. It was the only one with the red tractor seat on the cover, *Achille Castiglioni, Meister des Design der Gegenwart,* and contained photos of all the objects in his collection.

Yet the way he talked about them, the hasty, almost sloppy movements with which he picked up each object in turn, the light in an otherwise gloomy room, his smoking—it was all magical. Achille's energy was unique. Those hands! Those cigarettes! I pulled out my little black Minox 35 GT and with his permission tried to capture the moment in pictures. When I developed them later on, it turned out that they were all out of focus. Even Eadweard Muybridge's *Animals in Motion* were sharper! Castiglioni was so quick he was impossible to pin down.

Only after four hours did I finally summon up the courage to ask him for a job. He had no need of any more assistants, he replied, and suggested that I open a studio of my own instead. Well if that was what Achille recommended, then surely that was the way. I took the train back to Zurich and wasted no time in renting a 35–square–meter studio space with bay window on Hardturmstrasse in Zurich, right next to the River Sihl. That was my first studio, opened the day after my graduation, as it were, in 1991.

Bar Basso and Negroni Sbagliato — The Designers' Cocktail

Verbal Doodling

It was Jasper Morrison who gave me a token for the Bar Basso during one of the Milan furniture fairs. But the story behind it was this: James Irvine, a friend of Jasper's from England who worked at the Sottsass studio in Milan, had a studio of his own very near the Bar Basso. That made him a regular there, both during the week and on Sundays. The bar also hosted a group of regulars who had been meeting there for a Sunday drink since 1950. Traditions of any kind matter a lot to the English. My friend Martin Greenland, for example, makes a point of drinking a single malt whisky at 5 o'clock every Sunday. He also wears a signet ring bearing the family coat of arms, and is now the secretary of Europe's oldest sports club, the Sankt Moritz Skeleton Club, which is itself a product of traditions, customs, and history.

Anyway, it was James, Jasper, and Marc Newson who initiated the tradition of meeting for after-dinner drinks at the Bar Basso during the Salone. Towards the end of the 1990s they also organized a Wednesday-night party there that was reserved for designer friends only—people like Thomas Sandell, Thomas Eriksson, Andreas Brandolini, Axel Kufus, and friends of friends, maybe fifty altogether, maybe a hundred. It was beyond belief, that bar on Via Plinio: waiters all clad in classical garb with bow tie or black tie and white shirt, with or without a waistcoat or vest, a lady manning the till, and flanking her Maurizio Stocchetto, his beady eyes half hidden behind black, horn–rimmed spectacles. And then there was this incredibly large goblet that had been custom–made in Venice for Maurizio's father, Mirko Stocchetto, specially for serving Negroni sbagliatos. It must have held about a liter and the alcohol content was close to forty percent, or so it felt. Negroni sbagliato consists of one third Campari, one third vermouth, and one third champagne. No wonder it was so incredibly good–humored there! And the drinking went on until well into the night or even next morning. Once the official closing time came around, Maurizio lowered the shutters, allowing us to linger for a while.

After a few years, we began bringing along our assistants, too, and the Bar Basso on Via Plinio became *the* place to go for after–dinner drinks. The guests now came from all over the world, and not all of them were designers. Sometimes the bar became so full that traffic on the Piazza came to a standstill and it took ages for the cocktails to arrive. At least during the Salone it was a real institution and everyone's favorite haunt. As my work became more professional and my obligations to the firms I worked with increased, going to the Bar Basso the night before no longer seemed like such a good idea; but whenever I do go there, I'm one of the few who is served his drink in the famous goblet.

In 2002 I had a small show at the Asplund gallery and store in Stockholm and I thought how great it would be to fly in Maurizio Stocchetto, which is what I then did. He arrived with a sports bag full of his barkeeper's utensils, enabling us to serve up four of our own drinks at the opening event. Having a well–known Swedish vodka producer as sponsor was also a huge stroke of luck. That evening has gone down in history as the day the Bar Basso went to Stockholm.

Verbal Doodling

IKEA PS — La rivoluzione a Milano siamo noi svedesi

The design world of 1990s Milan was crazy, on a real high. Everything was possible and its charisma was spilling over into other branches of industry as well. It was during that time that I got to know Stefan Ytterborn, a Swede who together with his wife Klara had opened a design store in Stockholm. There he introduced his Scandinavian clientele to internationally acclaimed designers by selling them creations by Marc Newson, Ross Lovegrove, Konstantin Grcic, and others. The agency that Ytterborn had co–founded with Oscar Fuentes specialized not just in graphic design and communications but also in design consultancy, and he was the one who brought the *IKEA PS* collection to Milan. Given that the designers, namely Thomas Eriksson and Thomas Sandell, were the same as those who had done the *Progetto Oggetto* for Cappellini, it must have felt very much like an attack to the Italians.

This was the first time such an intermingling of different price levels had been tried out—and it was earth–shattering. The exhibition was held in a conservatory at the Giardino Indro Montanelli, diagonally opposite the Spazio Krizias and Hotel Manin. It certainly felt like a very public flexing of muscles and a direct challenge to the powers that be in the world of Italian design. Then came 1998, which was the year of the now legendary show *Living in Sweden* by a conglomerate of Swedish firms: Asplund, CBI, David Design, and Swecode, with food by Sturehof, music by Superstudio Diesel Music, fashion designs by Ellegal/Illegal and the fantastic magazine *Stockholm New* from Sweden. It was a different kind of event and in a very different style—calm atmosphere, cool music, excellent food. I was there all day long and spent a lot of time with my friends from the north and with Alberto Meda, Miska Miller Lovegrove, and Ross Lovegrove, who had driven us in his Fiat 500 all the way across Milan just for this event. There was plenty of room for the four of us in that dark–blue 500 Nuova—was a miracle it was, that invention of Dante Giocosa!

It was again Stefan Ytterborn who in the early days of the new millennium invited me to Stockholm and there introduced me to Rörstrand, then already part of Iittala (which in those days belonged to the Hackmann Group, but is now Fiskars). After ten years of working with the Italians, I was glad of the opportunity to gain some experience elsewhere. There was too much repetition in the south, which is why I thought to myself: "Let's go north."

Stefan is one of those very clever, crazy entrepreneurs, whom these days we would describe as a typical start-up guy. He ran a successful design consultancy until the age of forty, but then gave it all up to launch POC (Piece of Cake) to fill a niche in the protective clothing business—a niche that began with back pads for skiers and snowboarders and then expanded to include helmets and goggles. These days it's huge. On hitting fifty, however, he sold POC and founded CAKE, which produces electric motorbikes. He's highly intelligent and a good friend, to whom I feel deeply indebted.

His brazenness and pioneering spirit are qualities that are not nearly as pronounced in me. Yet you have to be at least somewhat astute and have some business acumen to be an independent designer. Lars Müller, who published Jasper Morrison's books as well as our Bruno Munari catalogue, once cautioned me: "Alfredo, be careful. Never rely on any one customer for more than twenty percent of your revenues, as otherwise you will end up depending on them. And you will no longer have the freedom to say no." As I had always been even more radical about this, and had chosen not to work for certain firms at all, I had never reached the maximum percentage named by Lars, even if Italy as a whole did account for a large chunk of my earnings. The projects in Germany, Spain, and Japan, and then in Finland, Sweden, Norway, and Denmark were consequently like a breath of fresh air, and at the same time brought me economic freedom.

Verbal Doodling

Amore mio, Milan and Italy remain my great loves

The Milan furniture fair always marked the end of my personal business year as well as the beginning of the next. Its impact on furniture makers, the presence of so many key people, the cocktail parties, the press—it had all grown in sync with my own advances into the world of design. But whereas my steps had been small and self–conscious, the Salone del Mobile and Fuori Salone had been striding ahead in seven–league boots and the global magnet for creativity had reached fever pitch even before the pandemic struck. What followed was a period of enforced reflection, in which the furniture fair could not take place and was obliged to take a breather, as it were.

Suddenly, people could meet only on–screen and products and innovations had to be unveiled at webinars. We rushed headlong into this new world, which did little to help our new products; and as very few of us designers are genuinely articulate (having never learned the art of public speaking), we were most definitely in new terrain. The whole thing became an experiment, now with thousands of participants, now with almost none. Egomaniacs flashed across my screen, but so did many an eloquent interlocutor. It was all very instructive.

Not being able to meet in person is as disastrous in our business as it is in art, which like design lives from people and is made for people. So the pandemic really was a big deal, even if it was also a time of reflection.

Verbal Doodling **Il consulente**

I often receive telephone calls from people I know from earlier phases of my life. My assistants, who perform all sorts of tasks for me and to whom I owe so much, have for many years acted as a filter that allows only certain inquiries to get through. I am also fortunate in that I still know the names of ninety percent of the people I have ever met. My brain is still working well, it seems, and my memory is sound.

One day I received a call from Alfonso Arosio, whom I first met through Cappellini in the early 1990s. He wanted to know if I would like to design a kitchen. Apparently, there might be an opportunity at Schiffini, one of Italy's most important and most innovative makers of kitchen furniture. Almost all its designs hitherto had been the work of Vico Magistretti, who to my great regret I never met in person. Hailed as "un gran signore architetto di Milano," he was as elegant as his designs.

The first thing I do on receiving such an inquiry is to pay the firm a visit. I like to sniff the air, check the chemistry, and form my own picture of how the company works. I also like to bounce ideas and to find out for myself whether the proposed collaboration makes sense. I usually know whether I like someone or whether a particular project, task, or firm appeals to me within the first few seconds. My assistants are sometimes alarmed by these gut decisions of mine.

Anyway, Alfonso and I decided to meet in La Spezia and take a closer look at Schiffini.

The two brothers who ran it, Dr. Carlo and Dr. Enrico Schiffini, must have been very young when their father died, leaving them in charge of his company. It was during that period that Vico Magistretti, as a friend of their mother and the whole family, not only took on the role of architect and designer, but also began designing Schiffini's stores and fair booths. To use today's terminology, he became the art director in charge of corporate design. No less important, however, was the way he played the role of uncle or ersatz father to the two brothers. As an architect he had built the Schiffini factory and designed the family's country seat in Tuscany, although his greatest contribution was undoubtedly his three great milestones of Italian kitchen design, the *Cina, Cinqueterre,* and *Solaro.*

So off I went to the factory, which is a real dream of a building complete with driveway and garden and a never–ending corridor whose blue doors were numbered using the font that Max Huber and Achille Castiglioni designed for their clock for Alessi. All three designers had been active in Milan at around the same time. Then there were the workers in production, who all wore the same dark–blue overalls with the Schiffini logo, the fleet of bicycles—also blue—with license plates, and the conference room full of furnishings by Magistretti, Castiglioni, and other classics of Italian design. It all had such class; everything, without exception, was in good taste, including the two *dottore,* Enrico and his younger brother Carlo, both of whom were now well beyond pension age.

And then there was the local architect, Giuliano Giaroli, who like Alfonso Arosio was a *consulente* or consultant. They were the ones who took over the reins after Magistretti's death in 2006, and it was then that my name had come up. So I took the train to Milan, and there met Alfonso and drove with him to Ceparana, La Spezia, *infinitamente chiacchierando*—chatting all the way.

Enrico Schiffini and I hit it off right away and were soon firm friends, though the chemistry with Giuliano made for an even stronger bond.

They also visited me in Zurich, which is always part of the deal for me. Inviting clients to the studio enables me to observe how they react, how they tick, what catches their eye, how interested they are in how things work. After all, the studio is a laboratory for investigating ideas and hence is very much a *Wunderkammer*.

Following in Magistretti's footsteps was a great honor for me, despite the enormous pressure it put me under—and the Schiffinis, too, most likely. But by then they had already endured years of uncertainty, and something had to happen. Being well over sixty, moreover, the two brothers were no longer on top of things. It is not that they were not up to it, but the market had changed and the competition was doing a lot of aggressive marketing, albeit without any real content. Furthermore, their "concept design," as Magistretti had described their stance, was beginning to look dated.

I offered to do a study, which basically means being paid for thinking! It was a way of getting to know them better and a chance to develop some ideas. The study turned into a deep dive, namely a full-blown research project on "the kitchen as the soul of the house." We built the Schiffini stand at Eurocucina and in

2004 presented a prototype kitchen in much the same way as the auto industry presents a "show car." The backbone of the booth was the kitchen from hearth to hob, with a paternoster, a cistern, a wooden vise symbolizing the kitchen as workbench, and all the fronts in copper. It was an audacious design, and a most unusual performance for Schiffini—a real dream of a kitchen. That gave rise to the industrially produced *Mesa* kitchen program (2009), and later to *Pampa* (2015), a kitchen with all-wood fronts.

I have seen all kinds of amazing production lines in my time, whether at Cassina, Moroso, Magis, Alias, or at Luceplan, but never anything to compare with what I saw two years ago, when Ferrari's chief designer, Flavio Manzoni, invited me to the Ferrari factory in Modena. And how astonished I was when Dottore Enrico, showing me round that consummate production hall, suddenly climbed into a 2-meter-wide drawer and actually lay down inside it! "The first coffin to be made of aluminum," he said. "You just close it, and that's that." Amazingly, it held! It was made entirely of aluminum, but with a glass floor, an idea borrowed from a local boat-builder. Never before had I seen anything as top-notch as that in a kitchen.

And there stood Magistretti's very own limousine, a Rover P6 3500 V8, with an interior by Cassina done in special leather, and an Alfa Romeo SZ Zagato. What a pleasure it was to drive my Ferrari 456 GT the 400 kilometers from Zurich to Ceparana, La Spezia, and from there along the coast to St–Paul–de–Vence and the restaurant and Hotel La Colombe d'Or, and next day to the Fondation Maeght, to admire the building designed by Josep Lluís Sert and the works of art by Miro, Calder, and Giacometti. I imagined Magistretti making the same journey. There was always this whiff of *joie de vivre* at Schiffini.

But what also fascinated me was the Schiffini factory and the precision of its production processes. With the two *dottore,* Alfonso, and Giuliano we talked more about food: how to cook beans properly, which beans are best, and which olive oil to match them with. When the conversation turned to canned tomatoes, it was of course those made by Giuliano's own mother that received the most praise. Henceforth, he would always bring me a jar of them as a gift, and when his mother died, he took over the tradition. There was a time when I saw Dr. Enrico quite frequently; and staying in La Spezia I also saw the Schiffini store that his mother had opened and run. She was actually the first to sell 1950s and 1960s Scandinavian design in Italy, alongside Maddalena De Padova.

Then the business suffered a downturn; not because of my kitchen, but because of the way globalization was changing the design business, demanding new structures, fresh investments, and new ways of thinking. Rationalization, production costs, and marketing all took precedence over quality; and none of us was able to turn the ship around. The change of management should have taken place much earlier. The complexity of this issue should not be underestimated. It has always been a problem for family–run businesses, as I saw for myself many times over in Italy—sadly. It is painful to watch.

But when we renovated our house fourteen years ago, Stefanie and I installed a *Mesa* kitchen in white with Carrara marble, which people still compliment us on even today. Schiffini quality really is outstanding.

Verbal Doodling

Giulio Ridolfo — Serene Radicalism, Radical Serenity

It was at Moroso in Udine that I first met Giulio Ridolfo, another *consulente* of the first order. We were standing in the prototyping department with Marino Moroso (also known as "Zio Moroso"), who was using a rapid prototyping model to produce a 1:1 prototype. His character, his personality, had made him a legend in his own lifetime, and because he spoke like a sculptor, even Ron Arad held him in high esteem. Regarding the shape of a chair, a sofa, or an object as a sculpture, Zio Moroso created sculptures for sitting on made of soft foam. And Giulio, too, clad as always in his couturier's coat, takes a sculptural view of things.

As a knowledgeable and experienced man of fashion, Giulio was not just Patrizia Moroso's friend, but also someone to bounce ideas off. He advised her on all things relating to fabrics, colors, and patterns, and on matters of taste, too. He has exceptionally good taste and knows all about fashion, pigments and dyes, botany, gastronomy, and world culture. Conversing with him is always a dream. He is always discreet, courteous, well-informed, wise, serene. Presumably it is this radical serenity—or serene radicalism?—that allows Giulio to sidestep certain questions and conventions almost entirely.

So there I stood, lost for words, happy, proud, but also surprised, since no one had ever said anything about production, and Zio Moroso had just gone ahead and done it. Patrizia, Giulio, Zio Moroso, two assistants, Patrizia's parents, the engineer Alberto Gortani, and I had gathered around the first prototype of *Take a Line for a Walk,* which had taken all of two weeks to produce. This was at Moroso's headquarters in Cavallico, a few kilometers away from Udine, where Giulio was born and, in those days, worked.

I was bowled over. What a coup! And all of this from a single three-dimensional sketch showing only the outside of a wing-back chair with footrest. It was a poetic approximation of a frame that aspired to be no more than a hint of an armchair. Zio Moroso apologized for not having asked my permission first, but said he had fallen in love with my idea, so how could he have done otherwise? As more and more people joined us, so the fan club grew in size, and once everyone present had had a say, it was time for something that was classic Moroso: pattern—making. Giulio, who had hardly said anything at all, took out his tailor's chalk (a flat square, 4 × 4 centimeters in size) and blissfully got to work on drawing the lines needed to capture the form in all three dimensions. Eventually, Giulio and I were the only ones still standing in front of the prototype. We talked about the options. "Even when drawing the first sketches for a project, I always analyze the touch that the chair or sofa should have: Should it be woolly or leathery? Rough or smooth? Because one gauge of a really good piece of work is being unable to distinguish between the material and the form." He then added another two or three lines to make it easier to pull back the upholstery. After listening to all the many different opinions for what had seemed like an eternity, this pattern—making went relatively fast. We were joined briefly by a seamstress and after she left went off to lunch, which as always was at a local trattoria, where the food was invariably excellent.

By the time we returned, the "dress" was finished and the adjustments had been made. That was Moroso—and that is still Moroso today! Whenever we designers are there for a visit, everything humanly possible is done so that we can see our creations right away. Hence that memorable visit to the prototyping department in Udine near Venice, which was also the beginning of a wonderful friendship with Patrizia Moroso and Giulio Ridolfo.

Giulio was also active as a consultant for Vitra and some of the other firms I worked with, such as Alias and Andreu World, all of which valued his expertise in colors and fabrics. He was bountiful with his recommendations, whether for boutiques in Udine or Milan, exhibitions, restaurants, or buildings and cities the world over. He always knew what he was talking about, and his good taste and experience could be counted on. For me he is such an exquisite person and such a great designer that I am constantly recommending him and promoting his work. I'm a huge fan of his. Enzo Mari appreciated this, too, and was always trying to make me his PR and communications officer. I always did my best to introduce friends of mine to other friends they might want to work with. With Patrizia Moroso and Patricia Urquiola, of course, Giulio was in great company. Together they formed a kind of "Bermuda Triangle"—except that instead of disappearing, their projects all but exploded.

And just as Giulio had helped me with my *Take a Line for a Walk,* so he assisted Patricia Urquiola with both her *Fjord* program (2002) and her *Antibodi* (2006). This was also the origin of the co–projects *Das Haus* for the IMM Cologne (2005) and the first project for BMW in Milan, with my friend Adrian van Hooydonk, chief designer of BMW. "The idea of *The Dwelling Lab* was to create a provocation, to defuse the automobile interior. Because there is always so much visual contamination inside a car. Yet you sit there for hours, forgoing the pleasures of your own sofa!" say Giulio and Patricia.

Kvadrat once asked Giulio the designer to come up with new color schemes for some of its existing collections, and after scrutinizing them carefully he changed the technology. *Steelcut Trio* was among the first to be tackled; then came *Canvas, Recheck,* and *Remix,* so that Giulio's work is now one of the supporting pillars of the Kvadrat collections. And deservedly so. Even if I myself designed almost two dozen fabrics for Kvadrat, his work remains unmatched.

Our friendship deepened as we were thrown together at the many banquets and dinners held at the design fairs in Stockholm, Paris, Copenhagen, and Milan. The delightful Soledad Lorenzo and her husband Mario Ruiz were also present at many of these fine dining events.

Alfredo Häberli

The mixture of Spanish and Italian to which those encounters gave rise would fill not only a "supplemento al dizionario italiano" à la Bruno Munari, but also a "supplemento all'ironia e all'arguzia."

But it is those same encounters that make the fairs so worthwhile and that are the essence of design—and of friendship.

Ramón Úbeda, Fearless Acrobat and Chameleon

Verbal Doodling

It was through my travels and constant pursuit and absorption of every conceivable source of visual stimulation, inspiration, and excitement that I discovered in Barcelona and Madrid two cities that reminded me powerfully of my native Argentina—and Spanish design as well! There was Javier Mariscal with his *Cobi* mascot for the 1992 Olympic Games in Barcelona, his *Duplex* barstool and *Trampolin* chair, to say nothing of the graphic designs he did for his new home of *Bar–Cel–Ona* (1979), his interior designs for the *Gambas* restaurant, and his comic–like style of industrial design that I discovered through the magazines *Madriz, Ardi,* and *De Diseño.* I spent a few days with Javier at the Hôtel Particulier Montmartre in Paris, where we were both on the jury for a Nespresso competition. There I discovered what a great sense of humor he has, how quick–witted he is, and how eager to challenge monopolies and all things bourgeois. He was exceptionally stimulating, and as a young designer he impressed me no end. As critical as Enzo Mari, he was also playful and mischievous, always fighting tirelessly for the same goals.

Alfredo Häberli

De Diseño and *Ardi* became important sources in my search for that other Milan, for Barcelona, and with it the world of Pete Sans, Óscar Tusquets, Alfredo Arribas, Pep Bonet, Sybilla, Lluís Clotet, and Mireia Riera, to name but a few. Then one day I met a quiet, shy, unassuming man by the name of Ramón Úbeda. He wrote for those magazines and had a hand in their creation, though whether as a graphic designer, a journalist, a designer, or an architect I cannot say. Perhaps it doesn't even matter.

"He is the ideal go-to man for companies in the design business, the perfect person to get creation to accord with production, designers with entrepreneurs. He is good at mediating between talented designers who have lost their way and clueless producers, and is of great service to them both," to quote another virtuoso, Juli Capella. "He campaigned relentlessly for the internationalization of *diseño* long before it was acknowledged to be the best way out of the crisis, and he was instrumental in pushing Spanish manufacturers to be fearless about working with the very best foreign designers."

Ramón is a chameleon and acrobat rolled into one. He is also a very good mentor and consultant for firms that have lost their bearings and want to reset their compass. He helps where he can and does what he does best, which is to write books, design things, develop concepts, and bring people and producers together. It was Ramón who brought me to Camper, to BD Ediciones, and, most recently, to Andreu World, and it was again Ramón who made sure they got the best of me. He writes like Pablo Neruda, has a mind as sharp as Enzo Mari, is as open and receptive as Ettore Sottsass, and is as much a magician as Bruno Munari. He is also a great friend and connoisseur who, like me, has lived and breathed design for forty years. Our methods are similar and entail observing, investigating, traveling, creating, and consulting, always bound solely by the task in hand.

Thanks to Ramón, my horizons have now broadened to include Spain. He was a great help here, in part by introducing me to Don Lorenzo Fluxa, the owner and founder of Camper. Fluxa is another wonderful man, "una gran personalidad, un Don Señor," and someone I hold in high esteem. Together we were able to design more than two dozen boutiques all over the world, from Paris to Shanghai, from London to Sydney, and even in my home town of Zurich, too. My parents lived in Barcelona for twenty years, so I often arranged a stopover there to visit them. Meanwhile, I was working with BD Ediciones on projects such as the *Ginger* stool and *Happy Hour* series (2001), or the *Los Bancos Suizos* program (2005). Then we went to Mallorca, and how we laughed on those domestic flights out to the islands! Oh yes, we always took pleasure very seriously.

Another highlight was *Camperto&ether*, a collaboration with a shoe manufacturer, which for me meant designing a small series of shoes for men and women, whose rubber overshoes earned them the name *Campermeable* (2008). The eighty cartoons that I created for my first Camper boutique on the Faubourg Saint Honoré in Paris in 2006 were a dream come true for me as a young designer, and a welcome chance to try something new. But I digress.

Whenever we met up, Ramón and I would typically exchange a few personal words before getting straight into the magazines, interior design, and the personalities that came up in *De Diseño*. Ramón was part of this new movement right from the start, and not only that: He is also a key figure in the New Spanish Design—the movement that stirred up such a furor in Milan. He really did know everything and everyone. How else could he have become such a profound connoisseur of creativity and such an outstanding patron of design? This is a position he has retained to this day. Just recently he received an honorable mention at the National Innovation and Design Awards presented by the Spanish king in Valencia.

Our paths first crossed just before the turn of the millennium, and we have frequently been thrown together since then, including in the books that Ramón has published, like *Sex Design, Inout & Friends, Conversation about Work,* and others.

Verbal Doodling

Eugenio Perazza, with Courage and Passion

"Eugenio Perazza is a force of nature who has succeeded in introducing a culture of high–end design into a field hitherto bound by tradition, and who in order to make full use of all the new facets of design culture first had to overcome conventionalism, skepticism, and resistance to new methods, technologies, and experience. His decisions show him taking care to respect and preserve local preferences, while at the same time consistently cultivating an internationalism far removed from all nostalgia and provincialism." That was the verdict of the jury that in 2020 awarded Eugenio Perazza a Compasso d'Oro for his life's work.

I once had a fabulous meal with Eugenio. It was at a local restaurant that served traditional country fare, which in Italy tends to be simple but delicious. My trips to Moroso near Venice were always a good opportunity to call in on Eugenio. We invariably had exciting discussions about design, technology, and much else besides. That he was able to offer us designers methods and technologies that entailed knowhow, investment, and risk clearly pleased him. He himself had reinvested all his earnings in Magis right from the start. Nothing else mattered to him. He staked everything on that one card: on innovation and the culture of design.

The many ideas we discussed included a combination balance bike and scooter, a house made of cardboard, a partition–cum–cloakroom, various chairs, and much of the *Mee Too* collection for children. But the first of them was a coat–hanger with handle (1997), which would have been a sensation had not Eugenio commissioned the tool to make Marc Newson's *Hercules* coat–hanger two weeks earlier. So it was too late. We still get on really well, though we never did do any projects together. There are no particular reasons for that.

Perhaps the fault lies with me and my inability to wait my turn—whether in a restaurant or at a buffet or anywhere else where I am just one among many. The moment I have the feeling that I will have to elbow my way to the front or stake out my own territory, I quickly lose interest. So that could have been a factor. Having said that, Eugenio never made me feel unwelcome, which makes me all the happier that he has done such productive work with designer friends of mine such as Konstantin, Jasper, and Ronan & Erwan—to say nothing of all those early works of James Irvine.

These days, Magis is run by Eugenio's son Alberto, an exemplary manager for whom design is a stance that calls for both cool unflappability and visionary fervor at the same time. The firm is anything but mediocre and has become an outstanding example of contemporary, innovative Italian design.

Continuity with Clients or Endless Lines

Verbal Doodling

One design a week should be possible, or so I thought at first. I also imagined a client list amounting to just five companies—surely that would be sufficient? The parameters in fact turned out to be extremely difficult to achieve in reality. For sure, there are companies for whom I have been working, for more than twenty years, developing eight product families for the one, twelve, or five for others. But how is continuity supposed to develop when during that same period there have been eight CEOs and even more project managers and strategic managers? I thought it would be different with family–run businesses, but after a couple of generations, they, too, run into the same sorts of difficulties. That is just one of the obstacles facing us designers. Any change in the key positions at the top and you have to start all over again. Of course, I am fortunate in having a few products that sell really well; but if sales like that fail to materialize, we designers soon lose our allure. And I haven't even mentioned the graphic designers and consultants. Continuity and all the human factors are what are most difficult to manage, and this makes constant personal and professional development all the more important. The practice of hire and fire has now become so widespread that there are designers who work for multiple clients and clients that work with multiple designers. Unsurprisingly, their catalogues are starting to look increasingly alike. Character and a clear stance, by contrast, are things that endure, even if they are difficult to maintain and are becoming ever rarer.

"A good project is not born of the ambition to make a mark, but of the wish to interact—be it on the most trivial level—with that unknown person who will use the object you have created," wrote Achille Castiglioni in Gianfranco Cavaglià's book *di*. It is here that the character, the stance, that an object can convey is to be found—not in some trend or market or in consumerism. And while that old trick of poking around in the archives and reviving the ideas of the past may be easy, for us "living" designers it can only ever be a warning, if not an alarm bell.

Mille Miglia, la corsa più bella del mondo

Verbal Doodling

"Alfredo, I have a gift for you, but one that I can only give you in the spring," said Adrian van Hooydonk on the phone, shortly before Christmas 2010. "First you have to do something for us," he added, "and if I like it, you'll get your reward." It was that typical Dutch humor of his that defined our friendship and all the many conversations we had at the Motor Show in Geneva and at the Villa d'Este on the Concour Élégance. Of course, I rose to the bait, whereupon he asked me if I could imagine designing a leather jacket for him—oh and one for myself, too? Yes, I could—and how! I had always had an affinity for fashion. It was my mother who sparked it. She used to make a lot of our clothes herself and even attended courses in fashion design; and my father, too, had worked in the business before he and my mother opened their restaurant. The jackets were to go with a classic BMW from the 1940s: a BMW 328 Cabriolet. And then I learned what my present would be: I was to be his co–pilot in the Mille Miglia. I was over the moon!

"Wow, Adrian, that's amazing! Thank you! Thank you! Thank you!" I cried. But then I felt bound to caution him: "You are aware…"—I began—"You are aware that you are asking one of the most expensive designers in Europe, and the best in Switzerland?" Silence. "And you are aware that the man you are asking to be your co-pilot is himself passionate about driving? I think we'll share the pilot's seat and the wheel." His reply was typically laconic: "I thought as much. It turns out that I was right on both counts."

The next step was to visit him in Munich and work out a proposal. Fortunately, BMW was already having its motorcycle jackets made by a very good manufacturer, so I could count on that. I got down to the work of designing and by May 2011 the jackets were ready: one for the driver Adrian van Hooydonk and one for the driver Alfredo Häberli. And to go with them I designed a sports bag and a suit bag to hold our custom-made overalls.

Car number 88 was white and was the English version with a right-hand drive. It was very fast and nimble and did not have particularly good brakes. The cockpit, moreover, was very small for the two of us. We met up the day before at the Hotel Vittoria in Brescia, where we were both staying and to which we would return after driving the thousand-mile race from

Brescia to Rome and back. The idea was to study the roadbook and receive our briefing, before sitting down to dinner with the other drivers of the twelve BMWs in the Classic category.

Adrian and I happened to arrive at exactly the same time and went straight to the bar in the lobby. We then did what we would have done at the Bar Basso and ordered a Negroni. While I was totally wound up, Adrian had more experience of these things than I did as he was a member of Munich's Gentlemen Drivers' Club and raced several times a year, sometimes with old models. Our glasses were soon empty and we ordered another round. I was still in a state of elation. More and more of Adrian's acquaintances trickled in, and lots of other people who looked very much like drivers—Mille Miglia racers. Both in an upbeat mood, we studied the roadbook and then went to smarten up for dinner. After dining together, we let some friends show us Brescia at night. The time just flew by. When we entered the lobby again early next morning, the bar was empty, but the entire crew and all the mechanics were sitting in the lobby, waiting for the drivers to finally finish their breakfast. We were embarrassed, but they thought it was cool, just like in the days of Piero Taruffi and Jo Siffert. So that was mile zero of the thousand up ahead.

We actually drove a very good race—almost as if in a trance. The right–hand drive called for some very precise instructions on the part of the co–pilot and hence for a good deal of mutual trust. The friendship between us deepened considerably over those three days we spent together. To this day, it remains the best race I have ever driven and we were among the top quarter at the finish. At one point during the race we met Marc Newson with his 1952 Ferrari 225 S Vignale and arranged to meet up for dinner with Charlotte Stockdale, Ilona Maniková, and Piero Gandini, whom I had known for many years through his former company Flos. Marc, Adrian, and I found many points in common and really enjoyed that chance encounter. The leather jackets were so widely admired that the following year they were produced in black for everyone. We again shared the cockpit, this time that of car number 101, a BMW 328 with a left–hand drive, and again met Newson and Gandini, even if only on the eve of the race.

As it happened, I had run into Marc at the Bar Basso in Milan about a month earlier. I had been following his publications and his works right from the start, just as I had those of Jasper Morrison and James Irvine. Among his most notable early achievements was the wardrobe called *Hangman* (1994), the *Super Guppy* lamp (1987), and the *TV Chair*. When Martin Greenland and I were designing the interior of the TECA restaurant in London NW1 for our friend Marco Bacchetta, I visited Newson's Coast restaurant, an ashtray from which I still have, and Piero Gandini himself gave me an *Apollo* flashlight. How wonderful to be so interested in technology and to be able to package it in such a tour de force of formal coherence! Marc is a designer of great integrity.

What impressed me most were all those watches he did for Ikepod (1996–2008). Among his most exceptional works were *Kelvin* (2004), which I was lucky enough to see at the Fondation Cartier in Paris, and his study for an automobile, the Ford 021C. That was a concept car that my car–designer friends did not take seriously at first, but that has become increasingly relevant as e–mobility has taken off. Such minimalism and archaism coupled with a distinctive aesthetic is something automotive designers could certainly learn from.

Only when doing the research for this book did I realize that the green variant was exhibited at the Spazio Fendi in Milan back in 2004. That is where ten years later I would unveil my

Alfredo Häberli

own work for an auto maker, my *Spheres—Perspectives in Precision & Poetry* for BMW. That work, like Marc's, developed themes that have since become major issues for car makers. My favorite book by Marc is his *Kelvin 40,* in which he gives his visions between dream and reality free rein.

Verbal Doodling

Hotel Speronari — l'albergo con vista stelle

Hotel Speronari's key assets are soon listed: great location, good value, a punishing climb up to your room after an evening at the Bar Basso (i.e. no elevator), super Italian, one star—or one and a half after they changed the curtains. But as a student it was the only hotel I knew, and being loyal by nature, I chose not to jump ship. It was my go-to address in Milan for over twenty years, both during the Salone and on other occasions, too.

My room looked out onto the church and was the only one with a terrace. There was no logic to the room numbers, and the corridors were so convoluted that you often had the feeling that you were passing from one building into another, with a courtyard and veranda in between. The corridors were full of doors leading to rooms or closets, and some of them even to toilets and showers, and the floors were tiled throughout. My own bathroom was a prefab plastic capsule in which to have enough space to take a shower you first had to swivel the washbasin over the toilet bowl. The hotel must have salvaged it from somewhere or other and installed it in the room by hoisting it onto the terrace. I think it was room number thirty–two—or was it ten? How strange that I can no longer remember that!

Most important of all were Carla and Maurizzio, the young couple who ran it. They were the ones who leased it and who manned the reception—together with Carla's father. Maurizzio was responsible for all things technical, while Carla took reservations and worked the fax machine, and her father made it all look like a serious undertaking. He also calmed everyone down when the football debates over Inter or Milan threatened to get out of hand. There was also a cousin who was a student and did the night shift.

After entering through a doorway that would have been too narrow for anyone with a large suitcase, guests had to ascend a single flight of stairs up to the first–floor reception desk. This was located in a small, windowless space that doubled as the breakfast room. I only ever drank a coffee there, as Carla would not let me leave the building without hearing some story of what had happened the day before—though Maurizzio was just as bad. We became friends, and I was always glad of being able to book so many rooms all at once. And they never raised their prices—at least not for me.

But having to climb all those stairs after a long day at the Salone was tough. Later, once I was earning enough to stay at a different hotel, my guilty conscience moved me to pay Carla and Maurizzio a visit.

Ascan Mergenthaler, who was one of Konstantin Grcic's first assistants and in those days was still studying architecture—he is now a senior partner at Herzog & de Meuron—called me one day during the furniture fair to say that he absolutely had to get back to Basel, but the railway workers were on strike and there were no trains running. He wanted to know if I was still in Milan and if I could help. I happened to be chatting to Carla and Maurizzio when I heard of this outrage, so I told him that he should stay in Milan. Hearing the gist of our conversation, however, Maurizzio immediately offered to drive Ascan over the border to Chiasso. There it was: *Italia, mio amore!* Five minutes later he set off for Milano Centrale—where in the meantime fights had broken out—and as promised took Ascan back to Switzerland. Those were my friends at Hotel Speronari!

And then out of nowhere, after all those years, all those nights, all those arrivals at reception, and all those departures at checkout—something happened that I had never thought possible. Carla and Maurizzio found a different hotel near the exhibition grounds that seemed to promise a brighter future and I never saw any of them ever again. Hotel Speronari stood empty for many years, until it was finally fixed up as the Speronari Suites, which still has only one room with a terrace looking out onto the tower of Santa Maria presso San Satiro. No other hotel in Milan has impressed itself on my mind or touched me as deeply as did Hotel Speronari.

Fiera Campionaria or Exhibiting as Memorializing

Verbal Doodling

Hotel Speronari was strategically located just a few hundred meters away from the nearest streetcar. As a student, and in the early days of my career as a designer, I was glad of the streetcar to the Fiera Campionaria di Milano. That was from 1986 until the mid–1990s, after which came the Fiera Milano City and later the Rho–Pero. My first time at the Salone, when being clueless I proceeded systematically from one hall to the next, I saw a lot of crazy things: a bed in the shape of a shell being sold by a woman in a negligee, and all sorts of different styles ranging from the rustic to the colonial. But then I entered the modern halls—the halls containing a very different Italian design—and was instantly thrilled with much of what I saw, even if only a fraction of it could actually be described as design.

That was also the location of the Campari Bar. This round building dating from the postwar era—these days it would count as modernist—with the Campari logo on the roof had originally been the German pavilion. When I returned to the Salone the following year I had a better idea of where to go, except that weekdays were reserved for trade visitors so it was not so easy to get in. As a mere student I was not welcome, though I still managed to smuggle myself in.

I once saw the presentation of an armchair that moved around of its own accord, as if performing a dance. Only later did I spot the men operating the remote control on a balcony high up in the hall. The design was by Gianfranco Ferré and Paolo Nava for B&B, and the idea was to create an armchair and sofa with a winter and a summer coat; hence the name of their program: *Gli Abiti,* "the coats." What really fascinated me, however, was not just the designs themselves but also the way they were staged. The stands were works of architecture in their own right: all those buildings, all the different characters that I met, the architects and the designers—they were all there. I was constantly looking around and trying to understand what I was seeing and what I was just then experiencing.

And then I found myself riding on the same tram as Achille Castiglioni and his wife Irma. How I relished that moment, since only I knew what Castiglioni had sparked in me. And only I knew that he was the reason why I was riding that streetcar from the Fiera Campionaria to the Duomo in Milan, heading for my hotel on Via Speronari.

Verbal Doodling

Ettore Sottsass or: the Inner Life of Restaurants

That my grandparents owned a hotel and my parents a restaurant is a coincidence that was to have a formative impact on my life and my character. I have often noticed that politeness and respect are somehow hard–wired in my family, as is the notion of service. Obviously, for the owner of a hotel or restaurant, such qualities are crucial to success, although architecture and food are important, too. Enjoying food in the company of others is of course part of everyday life, and Milan is exceptionally well endowed with excellent restaurants and trattorias. How many hours I must have spent in such places, making notes, reading, thinking, especially as my hotel room—except for the terrace—was not at all suited to such activities.

That is why I was constantly drawn to the Ristorante ai 3 Fratelli, the Bar Margenta, and the Boccodivino, which I first visited with Stefan Ytterborn. And I had more traditional haunts, too, such as the Ristorante Bagutta, or the Girarrosto on Corso Venezia, whose wonderfully simple cuisine we often shared with people from Alias or with Piero Gandini from Flos. Then there was Paper Moon, which we went to with Aldo Rivitti, director of Kvadrat Italia. There they sat, always at the same table, always on the same day of the week: "l'avvocato, il dottore, il professore, l'architetto, la signora, l'amante, i bambini e i cani." It was just as good for people-watching, just as much the theater of everyday life as a film by Federico Fellini!

A few times we accompanied Giulio and Jasper to the Alle Cucine delle Langhe on Corso Como or went to the Rigolo with Moroso. Sauntering along from Munari's place to the center of town, I sometimes called in at the Ristorante La Brisa, whose not so small, bright–blue calling cards with just a few deftly done strokes of white showed a chef with his hat flying off. That was in the early 1990s. The interior was bathed in a very pale, but warm, yellowy beige. The cuisine was simple but finely done and the service friendly. One evening I saw a young Asian woman there, and sitting opposite her an elderly gentleman with his hair swept back and tied in a small, thin braid. I wondered what the relationship between them might be and which language they were speaking. I could not hear it well enough and must have been staring rather too hard at them as the young "assistant" became visibly embarrassed. The man seemed familiar to me somehow, but it was only when he stood up that I recognized Ettore Sottsass. He greeted me politely and I eagerly seized the opportunity to exchange a few words with him. He was extremely friendly, and when I told him that I was from Switzerland and was currently preparing an exhibition on Munari and Mari, he seemed visibly delighted by the idea and even said a few words in German. Enzo Mari deserved it, he said, and such a show was long overdue. And did I know Bruno Bischofberger, a high–profile gallerist from Zurich for whom he had designed a house on Lake Zurich? Well I certainly knew the house; it stands all alone in a field above ours and I still jog past it even today.

Standing on the window–ledge of my studio is a black–and–white photo showing Ettore and Enzo together. What characters! What great people!

The Ettore of the Memphis period never struck a chord with me, perhaps because I was with Kuramata, Rei Kawakubo, or Zeus; but later I discovered other works by him, mostly the early works shown at the 2018 exhibition with Renato Stauffacher at the Milan Triennale called *Ettore Sottsass: There is a Planet.* Those early paintings, sketches, porcelain works, those first accessories and furniture designs touched me deeply, just as his sketches, his books, his writings still do today. I read his *Scritto di notte* more or less overnight. It is so beautifully written, so fluid and poetic—real manna for the soul. And even if there is something melancholy about Ettore's vision and trains of thought, his work is always bursting with wordless, but highly infectious energy.

If you were to add it all up, I must have spent a lot of time in restaurants in Milan. And during my childhood I spent more time in the kitchen than in the living room. Milan's trattorias and restaurants, bars and showrooms were my living room in the City of Design.

The greatest shock I ever experienced in a showroom was during that brief period when Danese belonged to Cassina or to the Charme Group and all its catalogues along with the entire archive, as well as all the stock in hand at the Cassina showroom on Via Durini, were sold off. There were books, objects, and accessories to be had for just a few lire each. I could scarcely believe my eyes. I did not have much money back then, and besides, it was not my style to buy things on sale. I found even the idea repellent. But I still bought the *16 Animali,* the *Pre–Libri,* some vases, and a letter opener. That it hurt nonetheless was for me a sign that Italian culture had become enslaved to the market and sales figures. Economically it made sense, even if I wished it would not (very few people understood Danese back then). My daily walk across the Piazza San Babila to Hotel Speronari was especially hard that day, both physically and mentally.

Alias would later take over Danese by doing a share swap with Cassina, after which it went to Carlotta de Bevilacqua and Artemide. I did two designs for Danese: one is the wooden bookend called *Pinocchio* and the other a metal dish, *Malvinas,* both of 1997.

Libreria Internazionale, Ulrico Hoepli — Libri illeggibili

Verbal Doodling

Another place I returned to almost as a ritual was the Casa Editrice Libraria Ulrico Hoepli S.p.A. on Via Ulrico Hoepli in Milan. There I found the Italian books that I had been unable to find at Krauthammer or the Zentralbibliothek in Zurich. Most of them were in Italian and published by Italian publishing houses. There were books about Franco Albini, Angelo Mangiarotti, and BBPR, children's books by Iela and Enzo Mari, and books by Bruno Munari, as well as periodicals and works about architecture and fashion.

My most cherished memory of the Via Hoepli is when Dottore Ulrico Carlo Hoepli invited Claude Lichtenstein and me to his home on the top floor of the building designed by the architects Figini and Pollini. Not only did the Hoeplis have Swiss roots, but they also had connections to the Museum für Gestaltung Zürich. Hoepli published the Italian edition of the 1993 exhibition catalogue *Unbekannt—Vertraut,* which in Italian was called *Sconosciuti e familiari. Oggetti di design anonimo prodotti*

Alfredo Häberli

in Svizzera dal 1920. I had seen quite a few private homes in Milan by then, but never had I seen such a beautiful rooftop garden and park as I saw that day. It was simply superb—like the beautiful books down below.

Those were the most beautiful, most memorable, and most valuable years of my life as a young designer. Milan had crystallized into an Ersatz–heimat that became dearer to me with each new visit, each new trip, metamorphosing into something unexpected and unimaginable. Every single day spent studying Munari and Mari, every new encounter, and every new conversation, it seemed, brought me just that little bit closer to my most important quest of all, which was the quest for myself and for the kind of designer that I wanted to become. It touched me deeply, as it still does today. It was also fascinating and gave me the strength I needed to keep going.

It was (and still is) a complex relationship that requires time, patience, and stamina, as well as goodwill and generosity, and a willingness to do the right thing. It was not just luck that helped me on my way, although luck was certainly part of it. It was also my natural openness, a certain fearlessness, and definitely also that joy that young people so often bring with them; and then something so precious that it is worth keeping: a touch of naivety.

I always succeed best when I am as close as possible to my true self. That is why I cannot offer any fail–safe recipes for others to follow—except to discover yourself.

Verbal Doodling

Eleonora Zanotta — Dream and Reality

The greatest boost to my development as a young designer came from two tiny things: one was my favorite toy car, a turquoise Matchbox Iso Grifo No. 14, which as a thirteen–year–old I had brought with me to Switzerland from Argentina in the shoebox full of my most treasured possessions. The car it was modeled on was designed by Giorgetto Giugiaro at Bertone, as I found out two decades later, and it was most definitely, and inexplicably, my favorite.

The second was the tag attached to each item of Zanotta furniture featuring a portrait of its creator. Those tiny leaflets measuring just 8 × 10 centimeters set the course of my life just as decisively as a sign for a one–way street—or better still an autobahn. From that day forth there was no plan B for me. And the one I have to thank for that is Aurelio Zanotta, who founded the famous furniture maker in the town of Nova Milanese in 1954. Is that how life works? Is it always such tiny impulses that define a whole life? Is that the key to happiness, as some would doubtless say? And if so, did happiness find me?

Zanotta certainly became my lodestar and its stand my top priority every time I visited the Salone. Without exaggerating, I can honestly say that I walked through it four, five, or even six times, hoovering up as many brochures as possible and examining everything very carefully. And then I began writing letters to the director. I wrote about the dream still closest to my heart, that of *progettare è un tappeto pieno di immagini*. I also took the liberty of commenting on what I had seen. My collection of references grew and grew, my most precious catalogue being the little booklet containing the whole collection from 1986/87 with Giuseppe Terragni's stylized, graphic chair on the cover. That little catalogue of 12 × 17 centimeters remains close to my heart even today. Then there were the brochures of the early 1990s containing the works by Enzo Mari. It was in part through my research for the Bruno Munari exhibition at the Museum für Gestaltung, to which Zanotta also had ties and in any case knew from its Achille Castiglioni exhibition, but also through my letters—and the good offices of Duilio Gregorini—that I became friends with Aurelio's older daughter, Eleonora. She was a passionate equestrian, but when her father died in 1991 willingly took over the reins at Zanotta. That was the year I graduated.

Alfredo Häberli

Although I never actually met her father, my visits to Nova Milanese and the Zanotta stand at the Salone had already brought me closer to my dream. My encounters with Munari and Mari, moreover, had yielded some amusing anecdotes that I was able to share with both Eleonora and with Daniele Greppi, who likewise had tales to tell about Mari. Daniele also organized fragments of Zanotta furniture for me, which I then reverentially displayed in my studio. The most interesting of them was the armrest of the *Daniele* sofa (1992) and the aluminum corner of the *Dongiovanni* table (1991). Daniele and I had some interesting conversations, as I was always eager to learn about the technical and engineering aspects of production. There was therefore a didactic motivation behind my requests to peek inside the factory, which for me was always a great learning opportunity, even if there were hardly any books. One of the few to be found was *Elegant Techniques, Italian Furniture Design 1980–1992, La materia dell'invenzione,* and perhaps *Mutant Materials in Contemporary Design,* which was a tie–in book for the MoMA exhibition in New York. The copy I possess is one of the ones with the special cover by Gaetano Pesce.

Every Friday morning, Eleonora and Daniele, who was in charge of the *ufficio tecnico,* set aside some time to meet young designers and architects, sometimes in the presence of the technical director, Fausto Benelli. That opportunity for young people to share their visions was a very beautiful and worthwhile tradition, even if it resulted in piles of unsolicited faxes. Presumably it can be traced back to the period when Aurelio Zanotta, who always had an ear for those who think outside the box, those who are unbound by rules, held an "audience" for architects from Milan.

For me, too, it all started on one such Friday. After several years of visiting Zanotta, I, too, was invited to present an idea of my own. That really put me on the spot. What should I show? It could be almost anything. But what did the Zanotta catalogue really need? What might make the perfect addition to the range? It had to be something that would not cannibalize their existing products—that was always my bottom line.

I imagined a shelf unit in the form of a narrow bench that could also be stacked up to form a bookcase, but as I had suspected, they already had something similar by Enzo Mari. Well, at least it was by him! Or was my idea not good enough? Perhaps it was nothing special? How can you be honest and candid without hurting a young person? How honest are firms? The fact is there is no other way: You have to expose yourself to criticism and censure, just as all writers sooner or later have to face the verdict of a publisher.

The next idea of mine was a good one, however. And a year later I was able to make the first drawings for a desk with shelf called *Ricreo* (1998), for the *Zurigo* sofa (1999), and for the modular sideboard *Florence* (2000)—and only then did production welcome me with open arms. In the course of time, Eleonora's brother Martino and sister Francesca also became involved in the business, which meant that the catalogue kept changing direction.

Following the vicissitudes of the market is of course important, but there is a world of difference between letting your marketing department supply information and letting it run the whole show. And if design is understood as nothing more than giving the market what it wants, then R&D becomes a mere tool and innovation falls by the wayside. The age of courageous manufacturers putting things on the market without knowing how they would sell, if at all, seemed to be drawing to a close. Even if only indirectly, I sensed that the market was changing and that businesses were becoming more and more defensive. The willingness to take risks had dissipated.

Design became more commercial and that it was now heavily influenced by marketing became ever more apparent, even in Italy. Sales figures set the course and both producers and their products began to look more and more alike. The machinery of trade fairs caused visitor numbers to skyrocket, and all that counted now was visitor numbers in aggregate, not the caliber of the trade visitors. The rental fees for stands and hotel prices went through the roof and the pressure to deliver innovative new products became relentless. Despite several initiatives by certain firms, the Salone management consistently ruled out becoming a biennale, yet the signs of collapse were already multiplying and we were still in the thick of it. All architects and designers of renown had—and still have—around thirty people working for them: ten of them for free for the sake of their CV, ten for just a thousand euros a month, and ten with certain perks, which is a standard model in the design business, but unthinkable in northern Europe. Designers, moreover, took to creating much the same sort of thing for everybody. The stock market peaked, allowing some people to become very rich very fast. The development that started in the early 2000s has only accelerated over the past ten years.

The research and vision that made Italian design so powerful in the postwar years and the era of the great patrons that followed from the 1960s to 1980s were beginning to look old, and many family–run businesses went into decline once the second or third generation took over. Perhaps this has to do with the Latin tendency to involve as many family members as possible, or with genes and the fraught question of whether the next generation really is the best option for the future of the company.

Italy's furniture industry certainly suffered an earthquake. Big names like Cassina, B&B, Arteluce, and Flos, and smaller ones like Zanotta, Alias, Luceplan, Cappellini, and De Padova went through a turbulent period of change. Some family businesses were sold to investment groups, others failed to find a suitable successor, or left the succession to the last minute with the result that it was poorly managed. Many had all their resources siphoned off. The same process is now happening in other lines of business, too, even though the Anglo–Saxon concept of the lean economy cannot possibly work in creative fields like ours. Those few family businesses that carefully set aside some of their profits in order to reinvest them later on are still functioning even today. The digitalization of the furniture industry is also advancing apace, but at what horrendous cost! There are no reserves and profits comparable to those of the fashion industry. Besides, domestic interiors are more important in northern Europe than in the south, where outdoor spaces often count for more.

All the big trade fairs—for the lighting and furniture industries, the automotive industry, watches and jewelry, and fashion—are having to reset their compass. We may have an inkling of where to go from here, but certainly not a solution. This is the new reality we have to come to terms with. We as a society are having to redefine and re-earn our prosperity. We are having to create new supply chains, restructure our economies, establish new business models, and develop new technologies—and all of these things at once. I personally would prefer to talk about hard work, inventiveness, and the pioneering spirit than about austerity, but times are changing.

As a father I often think about the future that today's young people face. I remember very clearly how things were for me at their age, and I would so much like my own experience to give them encouragement so that whatever their dreams are, they can still hope to fulfill them. I am very fortunate in having been able to live my dream and am deeply grateful for that. There can never be any one recipe for how to live your life or which career brings happiness. There is no right or wrong in any of this. But whatever happens, we all have scope for getting to know ourselves better, for asking: Who am I? Where do I want to go? What makes me happy? This last question will stay with you your whole life long. Of course, we are influenced by the input we get from others and from the more or less painful blows of fate. I used to think that every one of us was master of his or her own destiny, but these days am constantly reminded that that is not the case. When the Covid–19 pandemic struck, time seemed to stand still. For me it was a case of reality intruding on my time, interrupting my work, inflicting pain on my designer's soul. Reality itself had changed.

The Way Things Go

Verbal Doodling

I wrote this book during a period of reflection, when young people trying to find their path in life were very much on my mind. That I myself am currently in an introspective phase has to do with the cancelation of the event that for thirty-four years was one of the key stimulants of my life and work. And it was during that same thirty-four-year period that, still smarting from the loss of my home in Argentina, I found a new world. It was not just a lucky chance; it was destiny. I went with the flow and the flow swept me along in a way that in retrospect seems entirely natural. Another reason I began writing was because of all the young people I had working for me in my studio or was mentoring at design school—all of them young people facing momentous decisions.

That reminded me of the many meetings and encounters that gave me direction in my own life, as is much clearer with hindsight than it was at the time. All decisions require courage, because all decisions bring with them the risk of failure. This culture of failure, or rather of risking failure, is no longer so common, I notice. People are loath to appear weak, yet adversity is also an opportunity to show what you can do. That is why I like to talk of the "judo effect," by which I mean using your opponent's strength to gently disarm them. Life is like that, too. Acknowledging, accepting, forgiving are so vitally important, as is changing what it is in your power to change.

The stories and anecdotes I have told in this book each represent a crossroads at which I had to choose between two alternatives. Of course, there were many more such turning points than those recounted here. But the examples I give are inextricably bound up with my personal search for happiness. And if I have deliberately focused on Milan, then mainly because the furniture fair for once did not take place, so for once I had time on my hands. This was a new experience that saddened me deeply; it was both painful and depressing. Writing, however, fired my imagination and liberated me from my despondency.

Many of the experiences related here hurt me deeply and left scars—scars in my soul that have not gone away and perhaps will never disappear. They have rather become part of me, and over the years I have learned to live with them. Many of the stories are about the people I met on my quest to become a professional designer, who to my great good fortune were all wonderful people of great integrity, who became role models for me both as a designer and in my personal life. And just as failure has become taboo, so, too, has the concept of the role model. My aim was never to copy anyone's work, still less their mannerisms—which would in any case be impossible, since the design process entails such a high degree of complexity that any copy at all is doomed to be a poor copy. It was rather to admire and aspire to what they had become, what they had created, how they interacted with the world, and how they mastered and shaped their lives and the lives of others. As children we dream of things without really understanding how they come about. We simply want to learn, to play, or to grow up to be like a good friend or like granny. We laugh a lot and constantly forget time or do not register it at all. That is what it is all about: about the inspiration of others, about what others demonstrate is possible, or have already achieved, and then picking up the thread and going our own way. The role models I look up to helped me to stay the course, though it is still very much my way.

Another reason I wrote this book is because I feel so deeply grateful. I am especially grateful to my parents, who put me on this path. After all, the greatest good fortune is to grow up with parents and siblings, grandparents and an extended family who all show you how to live, who teach you respect, dignity, and humility. Yes, that is good fortune indeed. What we make of it, however, is up to us. Of course, personal circumstances are a factor and cannot always be controlled. When friends maintain that I have just been incredibly lucky, I insist that I have also worked hard for my good fortune, and I still believe that today. But I also admit that I am incredibly lucky in being surrounded by people who believe in me: my parents, teachers, mentors, friends, clients, and not least my wife of over thirty years and our two children.

Another reason for writing this book was therefore to pass on this hope to other designers and to all those who work in a creative field. We are all equals when we agonize over the meaning of life, but a life well lived is almost certainly the life with the greatest possible convergence between what we do and who we are. I'm not yet sure how my own balance looks, but perhaps that lingering self–doubt is what fuels my passion, just as it is my passion that fuels my mission. The rest is the craziness of design!

I have met architects, artists, and designers who in the course of their lives produced an unimpeachable body of work, but who as human beings were at the limits of the tolerable—impossible people, choleric, malicious, egomaniacs, and such like. Do you have to be like that to accomplish such feats? That would not be me. And Bruno, Achille, Konstantin, and Jasper are not like that either, yet have still produced world–class work. But the question still haunts me: Was I radical enough? I am probably being too hard on myself. My aspirations as a designer and as a human being remain, as does the fear that I will not live up to my own expectations, that I will not be good enough.

What have I done that is really, really good? How have my old notions of design changed over the years? And just as I chose to end certain collaborative projects, and even certain friendships, so my path, and my ultimate goal, is constantly shifting. I am in a constant state of change. Did I reach this or that milestone? And if I did not, was it because something else turned out to be more important? Family and children perhaps? A relationship? Honesty? Friends? My own guiding principles have remained the same: intrepid curiosity, an indefatigable spirit, persistence, modesty, fellow feeling, and a capacity for critical introspection. I have been relentless in my pursuit of my goals, though I have also worked very hard and have had to sacrifice other things. And if I have made design my life, then only because it has always been such a joy, and because what I have accomplished fills me with such satisfaction.

Another reason I wrote this book was because one of my best friends decided at a very young age that he no longer wanted to live, and because an incurable disease cut short the life of my brother when he was still very young. They were robbed of all hope, but did at least bequeath to me a determination to cherish every day, every hour, every minute in which I could be part of this world.

The happiness that found me was the happiness of having been able to make Milan, the City of Design that defined my whole career, an integral part of my life, and to channel its tremendous energy into my own work, both then and now, in the writing of this book.

Ftan, Feldmeilen, Formentera,
scribbled down and written up between
2020 and 2022.

Acknowledgments

This book is full of stories about the people who have had a formative influence on my life as a designer and my encounters with them. Only when I became the father of two wonderful children did I fully understand the true meaning of life. And the one I have to thank for this happiness, this sense of purpose, and the huge changes that came with it, is my wife, Stefanie Häberli–Bachmann. Our paths first crossed as students—of graphic design in her case, of design in mine, our studios housed in the same building, four floors apart. Without Stefanie's support, her deliberate scaling back of her own career, and all those years of working invisibly in the background for the good of the whole family—work that is rarely acknowledged—much of what I have accomplished would not have been possible at all.

Muchísimas gracias,
Stefanie.

My primary aim in writing this book was to call to mind and refresh my memory of my own indescribable, incomprehensible adventures and encounters so that younger people can have a share in them. After all, it was those same encounters that gave me the strength to write the book in the first place, which ultimately is all about people.

And there are so many people, so many different firms that deserve at least a page, a sentence or two, or some mention in this account of my life. Not all of them could be fitted into the flow of my narrative, and for that I would like to apologize. Even if this early phase of my life as a student and then as a young designer came about without my team, I would nevertheless like to take this opportunity to express my respect and esteem for my very loyal, wonderful assistants at the studio, and to extend to them my sincerest thanks.

Sincerest thanks also go to our family friend Ursula Eichenberger for supporting me and encouraging me to write this book and for editing it for me, and to Thomas Kramer of Scheidegger & Spiess for having confidence in me and for giving me the chance to see this project through to completion.

Finally, a big thank you goes to Aude Delerue and Patrick Roppel for working with me so creatively on the design of this book.

Imprint

Concept **Alfredo Häberli**
Editing of the German texts **Ursula Eichenberger**
Translations **Bronwen Saunders**
Design **DelerueRoppel**
Printing and binding **Offizin Scheufele**

© 2024 Alfredo Häberli and
Verlag Scheidegger & Spiess AG, Zürich

Verlag Scheidegger & Spiess
Niederdorfstrasse 54
8001 Zürich, Switzerland
www.scheidegger-spiess.ch

Scheidegger & Spiess is being supported by
the Federal Office of Culture with a general subsidy
for the years 2021–2024.

All rights reserved; no part of this publication may be reproduced,
stored in a retrieval system or transmitted in any form or
by any means, electronic, mechanical, photocopying, recording,
or otherwise, without the prior written consent of the publisher.

This book is part of the two-volume publication

**Alfredo Häberli—
Verbal Doodling. / 30 Years, Questions, Answers.**

and is not available separately.

ISBN 978-3-03942-115-2

German Edition:

ISBN 978-3-03942-114-5